50 Walks in

NORTH YORKSHIRE

First published 2001
Researched and written by David Winpenny

Produced by AA Publishing
© Automobile Association Developments Limited 2001
Illustrations © Automobile Association Developments Limited 2001
Reprinted 2002 (twice), 2004

Published by AA Publishing (a trading name of Automobile
Association Developments Limited, whose registered office is
Millstream, Maidenhead Road, Windsor, SL4 5GD;
registered number 1878835)

Ordnance Survey® This product includes mapping data licensed from
Ordnance Survey® with the permission of the
Controller of Her Majesty's Stationery Office.
© Crown copyright 2004. All rights reserved. Licence number 399221

ISBN 0 7495 2874 5

A CIP catalogue record for this book is available
from the British Library.

The contents of this book are believed correct at the time of printing.
Nevertheless, the publishers cannot be held responsible for any errors
or omissions or for changes in the details given in this book or for
the consequences of any reliance on the information it provides. We
have tried to ensure accuracy in this book, but things do change and
we would be grateful if readers would advise us of any inaccuracies
they may encounter.

We have taken all reasonable steps to ensure that these walks are
safe and achievable by walkers with a realistic level of fitness.
However, all outdoor activities involve a degree of risk and the
publishers accept no responsibility for any injuries caused to
readers whilst following these walks. This does not affect your
statutory rights. For more advice on walking safely see page 128.
The mileage range shown on the front cover is for guidance only –
some walks may exceed or be less than these distances.

Visit the AA Publishing website at www.theAA.com

Paste-up and editorial by Outcrop Publishing Services
for AA Publishing

A02038

Printed and bound by G. Canale & C. s.p.a., Torino, Italy

Legend & map

Legend

← – – – – –	Walk route	P	Car park
··········	Optional walk route		Cliff
– – – – – –	Adjoining footpath		Rock outcrop
—·—·—·	County boundary		Beach
☀	Viewpoint		Woodland
▲ 392	Spot height		Parkland
	Built-up area	†	Church, cathedral, chapel
●	Place of interest	WC	Toilet
△	Steep section	⛱	Picnic area

North Yorkshire locator map

Contents

Contents

WALK		RATING	DISTANCE	PAGE

Rating: Each walk is rated for its relative difficulty compared to the other walks in this book. Walks marked 🚶🚶 🚶🚶 🚶🚶 are likely to be shorter and easier with little total ascent. The hardest walks are marked 🚶🚶 🚶🚶 🚶🚶 .

Walking in Safety: For advice and safety tips ➤ 128.

Introducing North Yorkshire

If you were to draw a straight line from North Yorkshire's most easterly point, just north of Flamborough Head, to its most westerly, near Low Bentham, it would stretch nearly 100 miles (162km). From north to south is 65 miles (105km). The county stretches from the North Sea to within 10 miles (16km) of Morecambe Bay on the west coast. It is a huge area – England's largest county.

It is also one of the most rural, with historic York as the only sizeable city. Its two National Parks, the Yorkshire Dales and the North York Moors, occupy much of the two ends of the county. The Howardian Hills, south of the Moors, and Nidderdale, south east of the Dales, are designated Areas of Outstanding Natural Beauty. In its far south-eastern corner North Yorkshire also takes in part of the Wolds.

PUBLIC TRANSPORT ⓘ

It is possible to use public transport to reach the starting point of some of these walks. Railway lines radiate from York to Scarborough, Thirsk and Northallerton, Harrogate and Selby. Whitby is accessible via the Esk Valley line, which connects with the North Yorkshire Moors Railway. In the west the Settle-to-Carlisle line provides access to some of the most spectacular Dales country.

Buses, too, have become more user-friendly in the last few years and, in the summer, provide a regular service to many of the main tourist spots.

For more information call the national enquiry line on 0870 6082608 or look on the internet at www.pti.org.uk.

So this is prime walking country, from the heather-clad heights of the North York Moors to the limestone country that is typical of the Yorkshire Dales – a place of contrasts and discoveries, history and legend.

Walking is certainly the best way to see North Yorkshire. Large areas are unvisited by roads, and some of the best landscape is only accessible on foot. In the North York Moors the roads tend to follow the tops of the ridges, leaving hidden valleys and deep forest to be discovered. The east coast, with its compact fishing villages like Staithes and Robin Hood's Bay, and its towering cliffs, is best discovered from the Cleveland Way, which also takes you in a huge sweep around the northern fringes of the National Park. Here, too, are castles, like Helmsley and Pickering, and the ruins of great abbeys, like Rievaulx and Byland, as well as the great Castle Howard estate with its sumptuous house and garden. There are minor pleasures to discover, too – the crosses of the North York Moors, once beacons for travellers as well as memorials, for example, and the remains of ironstone mining.

Further south, across the Vale of Pickering, once a huge lake, is the very different landscape of the Wolds. Here deep, dry chalk valleys and ancient earthworks are part of the attraction – as is the timeless, quiet feel of this little-known area. Moving west across the centre of the county, an area of rich agricultural land dotted with market towns like Thirsk and Bedale, as well as the cathedral city of Ripon and the spa town of Harrogate, you come to Nidderdale and then the Dales National Park. Nidderdale is a tough landscape with reservoirs and the remains of lead mining – tough but spectacular. But for many visitors, it is the Yorkshire Dales that impress and leave such vivid memories. This is a landscape of caverns and waterfalls, of limestone pavements and wooded valleys, sheep-cropped grass and the gaunt remains of industry, now softened by the passage of time. Stone-built villages cluster round ancient bridges or surround wide greens. Huge crags – none greater than Malham Cove – and deep gorges – like the Cove's great neighbour Gordale Scar – will impress you with the force and grandeur of nature. Here, too, as on the North York Moors, you will be struck by the ancient place-names, many deriving from the Norse and Danish settlers who long occupied the area.

At all seasons, and in most weathers, North Yorkshire holds its fascination. Wherever you go, you can be sure of good food, a warm welcome – and great walking!

Using this Book

Information panels

An information panel for each walk shows its relative difficulty (➤ 5), the distance and total amount of ascent. An indication of the gradients you will encounter is shown by the rating ▲▲ ▲▲ ▲▲ (no steep slopes) to ▲▲▲▲ (several very steep slopes).

Maps

There are 30 maps, covering 40 of the walks. Some walks have a suggested option in the same area. The information panel for these walks will tell you how much extra walking is involved. On short-cut suggestions the panel will tell you the total distance if you set out from the start of the main walk. Where an option returns to the same point on the main walk, just the distance of the loop is given. Where an option leaves the main walk at one point and returns to it at another, then the distance shown is for the whole walk. The minimum time suggested is for reasonably fit walkers and doesn't allow for stops. Each walk has a suggested map. Laminated aqua3 maps are longer lasting and water resistant.

Start Points

The start of each walk is given as a six-figure grid reference prefixed by two letters indicating which 100km square of the National Grid it refers to. You'll find more information on grid references on most Ordnance Survey maps.

Dogs

We have tried to give dog owners useful advice about how dog friendly each walk is. Please respect other countryside users. Keep your dog under control, especially around livestock, and obey local bylaws and other dog control notices.

Car Parking

Many of the car parks suggested are public, but occasionally you may find you have to park on the roadside or in a lay-by. Please be considerate when you leave your car, ensuring that access roads or gates are not blocked and that other vehicles can pass safely.

Walk 1

Gristhorpe Man and his Landscape

A walk in North Yorkshire's eastern extremity, where prehistoric man lived and died.

•DISTANCE•	5 miles (8km)
•MINIMUM TIME•	2hrs
•ASCENT / GRADIENT•	249ft (75m)
•LEVEL OF DIFFICULTY•	
•PATHS•	Field paths and tracks, muddy after rain, 11 stiles
•LANDSCAPE•	Hillside, then flat farmland
•SUGGESTED MAP•	aqua3 OS Explorer 301 Scarborough, Bridlington & Flamborough Head
•START / FINISH•	Grid reference: TA 096796
•DOG FRIENDLINESS•	Livestock in fields, so dogs on leads
•PARKING•	Street parking in Muston, near the Ship Inn
•PUBLIC TOILETS•	None on route

BACKGROUND TO THE WALK

A little inland from the rocky peninsula of Filey Brigg, which marks the end (or the start) of both the Cleveland Way and the Wolds Way, is peaceful pasture and arable land bounded on the south by the first slopes of the chalk escarpment of the Yorkshire Wolds. It is fertile land, once wet with bog but long-since drained and farmed. The local name for this landscape – Carr – is from an Old Norse word meaning boggy ground.

Early Inhabitants
Some of Britain's earliest inhabitants lived around here – not, like their successors, on the Wolds themselves, but in refuges among the reeds and willows. Most of the details of their civilisation have long since disappeared, with burial sites vanishing under the plough. Fortunately, however, we know much about one inhabitant, now known as Gristhorpe Man, whose remains are now on display in the Rotunda Museum in Scarborough.

Gristhorpe Man
In 1834 workmen, employed by the local landowner in Gristhorpe, dug into a tumulus near the village. Under a covering of oak branches they uncovered a coffin lid carved with a face (which they later trampled on and made unrecognisable!). The coffin was made from a single oak log, with lichened bark still adhering to it. Inside was the complete skeleton of a man, more than six feet tall, with his legs drawn up to his chest. His body had been wrapped in fine animal skin, secured by a bone pin. With him were a bronze dagger head and a bone pommel for it, as well as a flint knife. By his side was a bark dish stitched with strips of animal skin or sinew. It is believed that he is probably more than 4000 years old.

You will get a fine view of Gristhorpe Man's homeland from the first part of the walk as you ascend from Muston on to the slopes of Flotmanby Wold. This is part of the long distance Wolds Way, which runs 79½ miles (127km) from Hessle Haven on the banks of the

Humber to Filey Brigg. If the weather is decent, you will be able to see the Brigg to the north east while, further to the north, Scarborough is clearly visible.

The Carrs

The walk descends along an ancient hollow way route, and on to the watery peat landscape of The Carrs, which are criss-crossed with drainage ditches that include the evocatively-named Old Scurf and the channelled River Hertford, which was cut in 1807. You will cross the Hull-to-Scarborough railway line by the former railway station for Gristhorpe village. The walk returns by field paths and tracks across Muston Carr and through Muston Bottoms to the village, which is worth exploring for its range of excellent vernacular houses, many built of chalk, with their typical pantiled roofs.

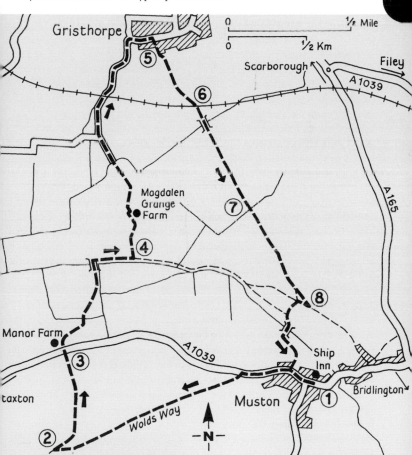

Walk 1 Directions

① From the **Ship Inn**, walk in the direction of **Folkton**. Just before the **Muston** village sign on the right, take a waymarked stile in the hedge on your left, signed '**Wolds Way**'. Go forward to meet a track, and follow the **Wolds Way** signs uphill over two waymarked stiles. At the top right hand corner of the next field go over a stile and continue ahead to the next sign post.

② Turn right down the track, following the bridleway sign. Continue downhill, in this hollow way, then across two fields to a main road.

③ Cross the road and walk through the farm buildings, bearing right along the track. Cross the river on a concrete bridge.

④ At the end of the bridge turn right along the riverside and follow the track to the next bridge, where you turn left up the waymarked track. Follow the track along the edge of the farm buildings. It swings right at the end of them and, at a crossroads of tracks, turn left towards the red roofed houses. The track becomes metalled and goes over a level crossing. Follow the road as it bends right into the main street of **Gristhorpe**.

> ### WHERE TO EAT AND DRINK ℹ
> The walk begins and ends at the **Ship Inn** in Muston, which offers bar meals and snacks, as well as traditional Sunday lunches. Just off the route, the **Bull Inn** at the eastern end of Gristhorpe village also offers meals and snacks, and welcomes children.

⑤ Opposite **Briar Cottage** take a signed public footpath to the right and go through a metal gate, then beside some farm buildings to a stile beside another metal gate. Follow the track down the field and over another stile, then half left across the field towards a railway crossing.

⑥ Go through the white kissing gates at the crossing, then continue across the field to two stiles at either end of a footbridge. Continue ahead up the ridge to a stile in the top right-hand corner of the field.

> ### WHAT TO LOOK FOR ℹ
> The soil under your feet will tell you a great deal about the **geology** of this easternmost part of North Yorkshire. On the first part of the walk you will find the light, dryer soils that are typical of the chalk landscape of the Wolds – sometimes chalk nodules can be found on the surface. By contrast, The Carrs has rich peat soils, in places almost black. When I was last here Magdalen Grange Farm was almost surrounded by an inky landscape, where the fields had been newly-ploughed.

After another small field go across a plank bridge and over a stile. Continue ahead with the fence on your right. On reaching the telegraph pole, go through an opening in the hedge and continue with the fence now on your left-hand side. Go over a stile and continue straight ahead. The path becomes a grassy track. Go through a metal gate on to another track, continuing to meet a crossing track.

⑦ Turn right, following the bridleway sign. Go over a stile beside a metal gate then follow the hedge on your left as it bends left. Follow the path along the field edge, go through a gateway, then across a bridge, through another gateway and bend left on to the track, which you follow to a kissing gate on to the main road. Turn left back to the village centre.

> ### WHAT TO LOOK FOR ℹ
> Visit **Filey Brigg**, the rocky promontory that punctuates the coast between Flamborough Head and the castle-crowned headland at Scarborough. You can explore the rock pools for shellfish and small marine creatures, and reflect on visits by Charlotte Brontë and by RD Blackmore, who set part of his novel *Mary Anerley* here.

Through Scarborough's Raincliffe Woods

Just outside Scarborough, a walk through woodland to the rare remains of a glacial lake.

•DISTANCE•	5 miles (8km)
•MINIMUM TIME•	2hrs
•ASCENT / GRADIENT•	584ft (175m) ▲▲▲
•LEVEL OF DIFFICULTY•	🚶 🚶 🚶
•PATHS•	Field tracks, woodland paths, some steep, 2 stiles
•LANDSCAPE•	Farmland and hillside woodland
•SUGGESTED MAP•	aqua3 OS Outdoor Leisure 27 North York Moors – Eastern
•START / FINISH•	Grid reference: SE 984875
•DOG FRIENDLINESS•	Can be off lead in most of woodland
•PARKING•	Hazelhead picnic site on Mowthorpe Road, near road junction
•PUBLIC TOILETS•	None on route

BACKGROUND TO THE WALK

The steep hillside of Raincliffe Woods overlooks a deep valley carved out in the Ice Ages. Although mostly replanted in the 1950s and 60s, the woods in places retain remnants of ancient oak and heather woodland – look out for the heather and bilberry bushes beneath oak trees that will show you where.

The Paths of the Aristocracy

The woods have long been open to the public, though in the 19th century they were privately owned by the 1st Earl of Londesborough, and some of the roads and tracks were named after his family – Lady Edith's Drive after his wife and Lady Mildred's Ride after her sister. Lord Londesborough was the grandfather of Edith, Osbert and Sacheverell Sitwell. Osbert recalled in his autobiography *Left Hand Right Hand!* how he and Edith were taken in the early years of the 20th century on hair-raising drives by their grandfather in his buckboard through Raincliffe Woods. They would then walk up the steep hillsides through columbine and honeysuckle. Unfortunately, they often became lost, and the Earl's language was, for a time, immoderate, until he remembered the children's presence.

Throxenby Mere

Beetle enthusiasts wax lyrical about Throxenby Mere. The last vestiges of the huge glacial lake that formed more than 15,000 years ago, after the Ice Age, it contains species of rare water-beetles, and is one of the places in the North of England to which coleopterists (beetle students to the layman) make tracks. You will also find the distinctive pinky-purple flowers and wide leaves of the broad-leaved willow-herb on its fringes.

Throughout the walk you will come upon humps and banks, depressions and pits that show that this hillside has been a hive of human activity in the past. As the path approaches Throxenby Mere it crosses part of a Bronze Age dyke system, while elsewhere are medieval

Walk 2

banks and the remains of pits for charcoal burning. You will also pass a small quarry which was used for local building stone.

The Sea Cut

In the valley below Raincliffe Woods is the Sea Cut, or North Back Drain, a flood relief channel that runs 3 miles (4.8km) from the River Derwent to Scalby Beck. Engineered in 1806 by local man Sir George Caley, it takes excess water from the Derwent to the sea at Scalby to prevent flooding in the Vale of Pickering. Operation is by means of a sluice gate (now remotely-controlled) 825yds (750m) west of Mowthorpe Bridge near the beginning of the walk. When in operation, it restores the Derwent's link to the sea that was lost when glacial deposits blocked its original route.

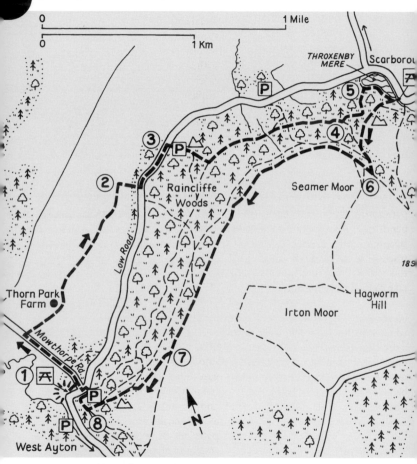

Walk 2 Directions

① From the picnic site, walk on to the road and turn left, downhill. After the woodland ends, pass houses on the right, then opposite a bungalow, No 5, turn right down a track to **Thorn Park Farm**. Follow the track as it bends left by the farm buildings, then right past a cottage to a metal gate. Continue to follow the track, which bends left then right, then through two gateways.

Walk 2

② Just before the next gateway turn right and walk up the field side to a stile beside a gateway, which takes you on a short path to the road. Turn left. Follow the road to the next car park on the right.

③ Go up through the car park towards the gate and uphill on the path ahead. Where the main path bends right, go straight ahead, more steeply, to reach a crossing, grassy track. Turn left through a gate and follow the path. Where it forks, take the right hand path.

④ Look out for a path on the left, which immediately bends right over a drainage runnel. The path goes down into a small valley. Turn left, downhill, then follow the path as it bends right again, past an old quarry. The path descends to reach

Throxenby Mere. Turn right along the edge of the Mere – part of the path is on boardwalks.

⑤ Just before you reach a picnic place, turn right through an area bare of undergrowth to take a path which goes up steeply until it reaches a grassy track at the top of the hill.

⑥ Turn right and go through a metal gate, then follow the path for a mile (1.6km), parallel with the wall. It passes through a gateway with a stile by it and eventually reaches a gate with a public bridleway sign.

⑦ Do not go through this gate out into fields, but turn right and continue in the woodland. Where the main path swings left and another goes right, go straight ahead, steeply downhill. When the path joins another go left, down steps and along a boardwalk to meet a crossing path.

⑧ Turn right and go down to a gate into a car park. Turn left on to the road, and left again to reach a road junction. Turn right, following the **Harwood Dale** sign, for **Hazelhead** picnic site.

Walk 3

Along the Coast at Robin Hood's Bay

Through fields from this obscurely-named village and back along part of the Cleveland Way.

•DISTANCE•	5½ miles (9km)
•MINIMUM TIME•	2hrs 30min
•ASCENT / GRADIENT•	466ft (142m) ▲▲▲
•LEVEL OF DIFFICULTY•	🚶 🚶 🚶
•PATHS•	Field and coastal paths, a little road walking, 14 stiles
•LANDSCAPE•	Farmland and fine coastline
•SUGGESTED MAP•	aqua3 OS Outdoor Leisure 27 North York Moors – Eastern
•START / FINISH•	Grid reference: NZ 950055
•DOG FRIENDLINESS•	Dogs should be on leads
•PARKING•	Car park at top of hill into Robin Hood's Bay, by the old railway station
•PUBLIC TOILETS•	Car park at Robin Hood's Bay

BACKGROUND TO THE WALK

Walking the coastal path north of Robin Hood's Bay, you will soon notice how the sea is encroaching on the land. The route of the Cleveland Way, which runs in a huge clockwise arc from near Helmsley to Filey, has frequently to be redefined as sections of once-solid path slip down the cliffs into the sea. Around Robin Hood's Bay, the loss is said to be around 6 inches (15cm) every two years, with more than 200 village homes falling victim to the relentless pounding of the waves over the last two centuries.

Robin Hood's Bay

For countless holiday makers, Robin Hood's Bay is perhaps the most picturesque of the Yorkshire Coast's fishing villages – a tumble of pantiled cottages that stagger down the narrow gully cut by the King's Beck. Narrow courtyards give access to tiny cottages, whose front doors look over their neighbours' roofs. Vertiginous stone steps link the different levels. One of the narrow ways, called The Bolts, was built in 1709, to enable local men to evade either the customs officers or the naval pressgangs – or perhaps both. Down at the shore, boats are still drawn up on the Landing, though they are more likely to be pleasure craft than working vessels.

In 1800 everyone who lived in the Bay was, supposedly, involved with smuggling. The geography of the village gave it several advantages. The approach by sea was, usually, the easiest way to the village; landward, it was defended by bleak moorland and its steep approach. And the villagers added to the ease with which they could avoid customs by linking their cellars, so that (it is said) contraband could be landed on shore and passed underground from house to house before being spirited away from the cliff top with the officers never having glimpsed it.

There was a settlement where the King's Beck reaches the coast at least as far back as the 6th century. Despite strong claims that Robin Hood was a Yorkshireman, no one has yet put forward a convincing reason why this remote fishing village should bear his name – as it has since at least the start of the 16th century. Legend is quick to step in; two of the stories say that either Robin was offered a pardon by the Abbot of Whitby if he rid the East Coast of pirates, or that, fleeing the authorities, he escaped arrest here disguised as a local sailor.

Walk 3 Directions

① From the car park, return via the entry road to the main road. Turn left up the hill and, where the road bends round to the left, take a signed footpath to the right over a stile. Walk up the fields over three stiles to a metalled lane.

Walk 3

② Turn right. Go left through a signed metal gate. At the end of the field the path bends right to a gate in the hedge on your left. Continue down the next field with a stone wall on your left. Again, go right at the end of the field and over a stile into a green lane.

③ Cross to another waymarked stile and continue along the field edge with a wall on your right. At the field end go over a stile on your right, then make for a waymarked gate diagonally left.

WHERE TO EAT AND DRINK ⓘ
Stoke up in Robin Hoods Bay before the walk, as there is nowhere else on the route. In the village there are several pubs and cafés, offering everything from a quick snack to a full-blown meal.

④ Walk towards the farm, though a gate and take the waymarked track round the right of the buildings to another gate, then to a waymarked opening beside a metal gate. Continue with a stone wall on your right, through another gate and on to a track that eventually bends left to a waymarked stile.

⑤ Continue to another stile, which leads to a footbridge over a beck. At a T-junction by a telegraph pole, veer right and take a path to the right of the bank. After 50yds (46m), look for a signpost for **Hawsker** in woodland. Walk to the signpost then follow it right. As the hedge to your right curves left, go through a gap on the right and over a signed stile, walking straight ahead through the field to another stile on to the main road.

⑥ Go right and right again, following the footpath sign, up the metalled lane towards the holiday

WHAT TO LOOK FOR ⓘ
At low tide, the bay reveals concentric arcs of rocks that are the remains of a large rock dome that has, over the millennia, been eroded by the action of the sea. The ridges are bands of hard limestone and ironstone that have eroded less quickly than the softer lias between them. Where the lias is exposed fossil hunters search for shells (among them the characteristic whirls of the ammonites) and larger sea creatures.

parks. Pass **Seaview Caravan Park**, cross the former railway track and continue along the metalled lane, which bends right, goes downhill, crosses a stream and ascends to the holiday park.

⑦ Follow the footpath sign right, then go left and follow the metalled track down through the caravans, eventually leaving the track to go left to a waymarked path. Follow the path towards the coastline, to reach a signpost.

⑧ Turn right along the **Cleveland Way** for 2½ miles (4km). The footpath goes through a kissing gate and over three stiles, then through two more kissing gates, past the **Rocket Post Field** to three gates by a National Trust sign. Go left through the field gate and past houses to reach the main road. The car park is directly opposite.

WHILE YOU'RE THERE ⓘ
Travel south along the coast to **Ravenscar**, a headland where the Romans built a signal station. Alum shale, used in fixing, was mined here in the 17th and 18th centuries and you can see the scars of the industry. In the middle of the 19th century a new resort, a rival to Scarborough, was begun here, then abandoned. The streets are still there, but only one row of houses was constructed.

Robin Hood's Bay and Boggle Hole

For a longer walk around Robin Hood's Bay, this extra loop takes you south to Boggle Hole and then back along the track of the former railway.
See map and information panel for Walk 3

•DISTANCE•	4 miles (6.4km)
•MINIMUM TIME•	1hr 30min
•ASCENT / GRADIENT•	328ft (100m) ▲▲ ▲
•LEVEL OF DIFFICULTY•	🚶🚶 🚶🚶 🚶

Walk 4 Directions (Walk 3 option)

After Point ⑧ on Walk 3, follow the route to the main road, then turn left by the **Grosvenor Hotel** and walk down the steep main street of Robin Hood's Bay – notice the alleyways and steps that shoot off at all angles as you descend. At the bottom of the hill, just before you reach the shore at the **Landing**, turn right up **Albion Road**, signed 'Cleveland Way'. By **Flagstaff Cottage** turn left up a flight of steps, following the Cleveland Way sign. The path ascends some boardwalk steps to reach the clifftop path. Where it turns left, follow the **Boggle Hole** sign, still along the Cleveland Way.

There are good views all along the coast, with the tumbled roofs of Robin Hood's Bay behind, and the bulk of the Ravenscar headland ahead. Eventually the path descends steps to **Boggle Hole**, one of the classic places to find the fossilised, tightly-coiled shells of ammonites. They are the remains of *dactylioceras*, a marine creature,

related to modern-day squid and octopus, that lived between 400 million and 60 million years ago. Ammonites vary in scale from fingernail-sized specimens to ones as large as car tyres. Locally they are known as St Hilda's Snakes, after the legend that Hilda, establishing her abbey in Whitby, found the place she had chosen infested with snakes. She used her spiritual power to decapitate them and then force them over the cliff into the sea.

Cross the footbridge and ascend the other side. When you reach the metalled lane (Point Ⓐ) turn right along it, leaving the **Cleveland Way**. Follow the lane, going right at a fork ('Unsuitable for long vehicles' sign), cross the stream and, part way up the hill, turn right up steps on to the former railway track at Point Ⓑ. This was the Scarborough-to-Whitby line, a 21-mile (33.8km) route opened in 1885 after 13 years' work. It closed in 1965. Follow the line, which crosses a lane and eventually reaches a main road. Turn right along the road, and after 100yds (91m) turn left, signed to 'Village', which comes back to the car park at Point ① on Walk 3.

Walk 5

Dracula's Whitby

Through Whitby town to see the inspiration for Bram Stoker's classic.

·DISTANCE·	4 miles (6.4km)
·MINIMUM TIME·	2hrs
·ASCENT / GRADIENT·	256ft (78m) ▲▲ ▲▲ ▲
·LEVEL OF DIFFICULTY·	🚶 🚶🚶 🚶🚶
·PATHS·	Coastal and field paths, then town pavements, 2 stiles
·LANDSCAPE·	Old town clustered around harbour and steep cliffs
·SUGGESTED MAP·	aqua3 OS Outdoor Leisure 27 North York Moors – Eastern
·START / FINISH·	Grid reference: NZ 905113
·DOG FRIENDLINESS·	Dogs should be on lead in town
·PARKING·	Main Abbey Car Park to east of the Abbey
·PUBLIC TOILETS·	At Whitby Abbey and (signed) in town centre

Walk 5 **Directions**

Three of the most significant chapters of Bram Stoker's *Dracula*, first published in 1897, are set in Whitby. This walk takes you to some of the places where the dramatic tale is set.

From the car park, walk up the road towards the **Abbey**. Go right at the **Cleveland Way** sign, through a gate at the coastline and right along the path. From this part of the coast you can look out to sea and imagine the stormy night on which the Russian schooner *Demeter*, steered by a corpse lashed to the wheel and with its strange cargo of boxes of earth, approached Whitby harbour.

Near the National Trust **Saltwick Nab** sign leave the coast along a caravan site road and walk past the **Galleon Inn**. Where the Cleveland Way continues ahead, bear right, following the road. Just before a telegraph pole on the left, turn right to a waymarked stile and follow waymarks through three fields and

over a stile on to the road. Cross it and turn left. At the end of the wall take a path to the right, following the line of telegraph poles and passing through a kissing gate into a lane. When the lane swings right go ahead beside a fence to a road. The town and harbour of Whitby are below: 'The River Esk runs through a deep valley which broadens out as it comes near the harbour… The houses of the old town are all red-roofed, and seem piled up one over the other anyhow,' wrote Stoker.

Cross and go down the road opposite, swinging right into **The Ropery**. Turn left down a cobbled slope to descend to a road. Turn right, then left just after the car

---

WHERE TO EAT AND DRINK ⓘ

As you'd expect of a thriving tourist town, Whitby has all manner of pubs, restaurants and cafés, catering for every taste. If you want to sample that seaside favourite, fish and chips, the place to go is the **Magpie Café** near the harbour. Although in the season you are very likely to find queues, the food's worth waiting for.

Walk 5

band of light as sharp as a sword
cut' Mina saw Lucy. 'Something
dark stood behind the seat where
the white figure shone, and bent
over it,' and she rushed headlong
through the town to save her friend.

Descend through the **Whalebone
Arch** on to the road. Turn left and
go down to the harbour and back
over the bridge. Just beyond, turn
left down **Sandgate** and on to the
Market Place, passing left of the
Town Hall, and turning left along
Church Street. As it bends right, go
straight ahead to Tate Hill Pier. This
is where Dracula's ship the *Demeter*
crashed and from where 'an
immense dog sprang up on deck…
and jumped from the bow…',
before running off up the street.

park, past the **Captain Cook
Memorial Museum**. At the end,
turn left and go over the bridge
then right along the quayside.
Where the road bends left, turn left
up a steep narrow lane, turning
right at the top. When you reach the
summit, **East Crescent** is to your
left. Mina Murray was spending her
summer in a house here with Lucy
Westenra, one of Dracula's victims.

Take the steps on the right to find
the **Bram Stoker Memorial seat**
(the right-hand one on the terrace)
from where the town is laid out
below you. On the opposite cliff are
the Abbey and the old parish
church, where at night, in 'a narrow

Follow the road round into
Sandside, and climb the 199 steps,
up which Mina ran to save Lucy
from Dracula, to the churchyard.
The seat where Mina saw
'something long and black bending
over the half-reclining figure' of
Lucy was on the north side of the
church, in the shelter of the
transept. Nearby, Stoker wrote, was
the grave of a suicide, where the
Count spent his days in Whitby.
Leave the churchyard by the iron
gate at the far end, bearing left past
the **Abbey** to the car park.

Walk 6

Early Warnings at Fylingdales and Lilla Cross

The past and the future come together on the North Yorkshire coast.

•DISTANCE•	7½ miles (12km)
•MINIMUM TIME•	2hrs 30min
•ASCENT / GRADIENT•	642ft (196m) ▲▲ ▲ ▲
•LEVEL OF DIFFICULTY•	🚶🚶 🚶🚶 🚶🚶
•PATHS•	Forest tracks and moorland paths, 3 stiles
•LANDSCAPE•	Pine forest and heather moorland, with views to sea
•SUGGESTED MAP•	aqua3 OS Outdoor Leisure 27 North York Moors – Eastern
•START / FINISH•	Grid reference: SX 106836
•DOG FRIENDLINESS•	Dogs should be on leads
•PARKING•	May Beck car park, beside stream
•PUBLIC TOILETS•	None on route

BACKGROUND TO THE WALK

Newton House Plantation is one of the many blocks of forestry that make up the North York Moors Forest. There are more than 50,000 acres (20,250ha) of trees in the National Park, many of them, like Newton House, open for walkers. Nearly three-quarters of the timber they produce is used for sawlogs, and the rest for pulp and other products. Look out on the forest tracks for deer, and for siskins and crossbills that nest in the plantations. And keep an eye out, too, for mountain bikers, who are encouraged to use the trails.

Crossing the Moors

Unlike in most of upland Britain, the most important of the roads and tracks in the North York Moors follow the ridges between the valleys. The tracks are often marked by standing stones or crosses, many of them of great antiquity. Although many are called 'cross', most are just a base or the stump – and sometimes there's nothing to see at all. The North York Moors National Park has Ralph Cross, one of the most distinctive, as its symbol and, after the forest section, our walk passes what is left of York Cross and Ann's Cross, with the remains of John Cross to guide us on the final descent from the moors.

Lilla's Early Warning

The most impressive and most ancient of the Moor's crosses is Lilla, which commemorates a selfless deed of bravery in AD 626. King Edwin of Northumbria, whose wife Ethelburga was a Christian, was the intended victim of an assassination attempt at his court by the River Derwent near Stamford Bridge. The assassin, sent by the King of the West Saxons, lunged at Edwin with a poisoned dagger. Lilla, a Christian and one of Edwin's counsellors, leapt forward to protect the King and was killed. Edwin had his body buried in the Bronze Age howe on the moors in sight of the sea, and had a cross, said to be the oldest Christian memorial in the North, erected in his memory. It still survives, despite a peripatetic life in the 20th century – threatened by shells from artillery ranges, it was removed to a spot by the Whitby road by the Royal Engineers in 1952. It returned home again ten years later.

Fylingdales – Another Warning

Dominating the middle section of the walk is the improbably large sandcastle that houses the Fylingdales early warning system. It's heavily fenced and there are forbidding notices at all approaches, but from a distance it's impressive enough. It replaced the three 'Golf Balls' that became one of the sights of the Moors from the 1960s. Unlike those unexpected but satisfying spheres, the new monuments seem not yet to have been taken to visitors' hearts.

Walk 6 **Directions**

① Walk up the wide track opposite the approach road. Where the track bends round to the right, go left down a signed footpath and descend to go over a bridge and continue along the green track. Go through a kissing gate and up the valley, eventually swinging away from the stream and into the forest.

② On reaching a forest road turn right, passing a flooded quarry on your right. At the next junction of forest roads bear right. After about ½ mile (800m), look for a broad ride to the left, with a white bicycle waymark by it.

③ Go up the ride, leaving the forest, and out on to moorland. Continue past the base and shaft of **York Cross**. Pass a track going left

Walk 6

and continue until you reach a waymarked (bridleway) post, where you turn sharp left.

④ Walk along the track, past **Foster Howes**, and continue with the fence on your right. Pass **Ann's Cross** to your right and ½ mile (800m) beyond you'll reach a T-junction, where you turn right and continue along the bridleway.

⑤ When you reach a crossroads with a signpost, turn right along the track to visit **Lilla Cross**, which can be seen a little way away. After visiting the cross, return to the crossroads, and go straight ahead, following the **Robin Hood's Bay** sign. The path goes parallel with the forest edge.

> **WHERE TO EAT AND DRINK** ⓘ
> May Beck car park usually boasts an ice cream van in the summer season, but otherwise you'll need to visit nearby Goathland or other local villages to find refreshments.

⑥ Go right when you reach a post with the number 9 on it. Pass posts 8 and 7, going left when you reach a trail sign.

⑦ Pass post 6, (by the remains of **John Cross**) and go through a gate, to continue walking downhill on a track. When you reach a yellow waymarker leave the track and walk

> **WHILE YOU'RE THERE** ⓘ
> Take the steep road starting on the B1416, near the access road to May Beck Car Park, that goes down into the deep valley the beck has carved out of the hills. In the valley bottom is the pretty village of **Littlebeck**, surrounded by woods at the entrance to a narrow gorge. The 29ft (9m) waterfall called **Falling Foss** in the gorge, can be reached both from Littlebeck and from the May Beck Car Park.

down to the left until you get to a waymarked stile near the ruins of a building.

⑧ Go to the left of the ruined building and make for another stile. Follow the obvious footpath downhill through the bracken, passing two public footpath signs, and over another wooden stile to reach the road. Turn left to return to the start.

> **WHAT TO LOOK FOR** ⓘ
> Forests are changing landscapes, with areas being clear felled and others newly planted. While this can sometimes make walking confusing, when wooded glades give way to an open landscape of tiny netted trees, it can have positive benefits for wildlife. If you are near a felled area towards dusk, you may be rewarded by the 'churring' sound of the nightjar. Virtually invisible in the day, when it sits disguised by its plumage amongst fallen leaves and twigs, it favours such open areas for nesting. Nightjars migrate from Africa in the spring, and lay their eggs in dead bracken in May and June. Also known as goatsuckers, as they were thought to milk goats with their beaks, making the goats go blind, they are said to carry in them the souls of unbaptised dead children.

A Walk on the Wolds

From the hidden village of Thixendale over chalk hills and through typical dry valleys.

•DISTANCE•	4 miles (6.4km)
•MINIMUM TIME•	2hrs
•ASCENT / GRADIENT•	459ft (140m)
•LEVEL OF DIFFICULTY•	
•PATHS•	Clear tracks and field paths, 9 stiles
•LANDSCAPE•	Deep, dry valleys and undulating farm land
•SUGGESTED MAP•	aqua3 OS Explorer 300 Howardian Hills & Malton
•START / FINISH•	Grid reference: SE 842611
•DOG FRIENDLINESS•	Keep dogs on leads
•PARKING•	Thixendale village street near the church
•PUBLIC TOILETS•	None on route

BACKGROUND TO THE WALK

Chalk underlies the Yorkshire Wolds. Unlike the harder rocks of the dales and the moors, the Wolds chalk is soft and permeable, so the landscape around here is one of rounded hills and deep dry valleys. These were formed when the meltwater from the Ice Age glaciers rushed with tremendous force across the chalk. Our walk is through rich farming land – indeed, these slopes have been cultivated since Neolithic people cleared them and set up home here more than 5,000 years ago.

Going the Wolds Way
More than half the walk follows the Wolds Way, a 79 mile (127km) National Trail that runs from the great bridge over the Humber Estuary to Filey Brigg. At its northern end it links with the Cleveland Way and at the southern end (via the Humber Bridge) with the Viking Way to Oakham in Rutland. Less frequented than many of the other National Trails, it offers consistently fine views and a wealth of archaeological interest along its pastoral route – as well as some very welcoming pubs. For much of the walk, too, you will be following the Centenary Way, a route established by North Yorkshire County Council in 1989 to mark 100 years of local government.

Sixteen or Sigstein?
Some say that Thixendale is named from the six dry valleys that meet here. The more imaginative reckon to count sixteen converging dales. Place name dictionaries, more prosaically, derive it from a Viking called Sigstein. Whatever its origin, Thixendale is one of the most remote of the Wolds villages, approached from every direction by deep, winding dry valleys between steep chalk escarpments. It has a number of old cottages, but much of its character is due to local landowner Sir Tatton Sykes in the later part of the 19th century. As well as building estate cottages, he contributed the church, the school and the former vicarage, picturesquely designed by architect George Edmund Street. Do visit the church – the stained glass, by Clayton and Bell showing the *Days of Creation* is great fun, especially the flamingos and the fearsome waterspout.

The Eccentric Baronet

Sir Tatton Sykes, 5th Baronet of Sledmere House, was a great church-builder and philanthropist – and an even greater eccentric. He insisted that his body needed to maintain an even temperature, and was known to stick his bare feet out of the windows of railway carriages to make sure. As he warmed up on his walks he would shed clothing, paying local boys to return it to the house. He even wore two pairs of trousers to preserve the decencies as he divested himself. Flowers were a great hate; he had the estate gardens ploughed up and told his tenants that the only kind of flowers they could grow were cauliflowers.

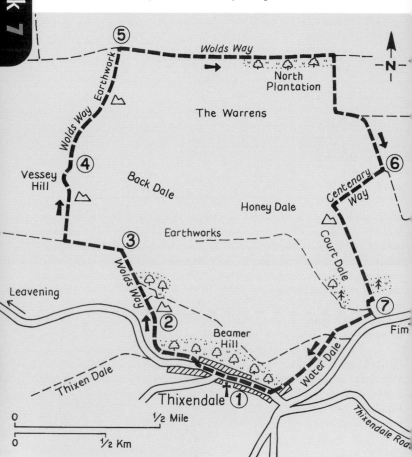

Walk 7 Directions

① From the church, walk west along **Thixendale's** village street. Just beyond the last house on the right, go up a track, following the **Wolds Way/Centenary Way** sign. Cross over a ladder stile in a wire fence on your right and continue walking up the track as it curves round past the television aerial.

② As you approach the top of the hill, watch out on the left for a **Wolds Way** sign, which takes you left along a grassy track. Go over a ladder stile then along the field side to meet the track again. Continue straight ahead.

Walk 7

③ At the next **Wolds Way** sign go over a stile and continue with the wire fence on your left. At the top of the field go right by the sign. The path descends to reach a wooden ladder stile and descends steeply into a dry valley to another waymarked stile, then curves to descend to a stile by a gate.

④ Follow the blue public bridleway sign to the right, winding left up the side valley. Near the top of the valley is a deep earthwork ditch; cross over a stile and continue along the edge of the field. Where the footpath divides go right through the patch of woodland on to a track by a signpost.

⑤ Turn right and follow the **Wolds Way** sign. Follow this clear track for ¾ mile (1.2km). At the end of the woodland on your right, look out for a signpost. Turn right here, now

following the **Centenary Way**, going down the edge of the field and passing a ruined building with a tall chimney. Follow the winding footpath past a signpost.

⑥ At the next signpost turn right off the track, signed '**Centenary Way**'. Walk down the field side on a grassy track. At the field end leave the track and go through a waymarked gate. The path goes left and passes along the hillside to descend to a stile beside a gate.

⑦ Follow the yellow waymark straight ahead across the field, to pass over a track up the hillside left of the row of trees. The path descends to the village **cricket field** on the valley floor. Go over a stile by a gate, on to a lane by a house. When you reach the main road, turn right back to the start.

Walk 8

Mallyan Spout and Goathland's Moorland

From the popular moorland village with its television links, through woodland and over the moor.

•DISTANCE•	4½ miles (7.2km)
•MINIMUM TIME•	2hrs
•ASCENT / GRADIENT•	557ft (167m) ▲▲▲
•LEVEL OF DIFFICULTY•	🚶🚶 🚶🚶 🚶
•PATHS•	Streamside tracks, field and moorland paths, 2 stiles
•LANDSCAPE•	Deep, wooded valley, farmland and open moorland
•SUGGESTED MAP•	aqua3 OS Outdoor Leisure 27 North York Moors – Eastern
•START / FINISH•	Grid reference: NZ 827007
•DOG FRIENDLINESS•	Dogs should be on leads
•PARKING•	West end of Goathland village, near church
•PUBLIC TOILETS•	Goathland village

BACKGROUND TO THE WALK

Goathland is one of the most popular destinations for visitors to the North York Moors National Park. Its situation, around a large open common, criss-crossed by tracks and kept closely cropped by grazing sheep, has always been attractive. Today, however, many tourists are drawn to Goathland because it is used for the fictitious village of Aidensfield, setting for the popular television series *Heartbeat*. The Goathland Story exhibition tells the village's history from the time it was an Iron Age centre for making stone querns to grind corn, to today – and there's a special Heartbeat collection of actual props and photographs from the series.

Spouting About Mallyan

The walk begins with a visit to the 70ft (21m) Mallyan Spout waterfall into the West Beck. At this point the valley carved by the beck has a lip of much harder stone, and the little stream coming from the heather moorland above has been unable to carve its way through. In dry weather only a trickle of water may fall from the side of the gorge into the stream below – which accounts for its name of 'Spout' rather than 'Force' – but after rain it can become an impressive torrent. Take care at all times – and be aware that sometimes it may be impossible to pass the waterfall on the streamside path.

Grouse and Heather

After you have crossed the ford and turned on to the moorland by Hunt House, you are likely to find yourself accompanied by the sudden flutter of red grouse as they rise from their nesting sites on the heather moorland. They feed on the young shoots of heather, so the North York Moors, which have the largest area of heather moorland south of the Scottish border, are an ideal nesting ground for them. If you visit in the late summer, the moors will be clothed in the purple of the ling heather: patches of the rarer bell heather with its flowers of a deeper purple, and the rose-pink cross-leaved heather, flower rather earlier. Sheep grazing has for centuries been the traditional way of managing the moors; the animals help keep the heather short and encourage the new shoots. Otherwise, bracken, the pernicious opportunistic invader, will rapidly take over as much as 300 acres (121.5ha) in a single year if left unchecked. To regenerate the heather, landowners regularly use carefully-controlled burning in the early spring or the autumn when the ground is wet. The fire burns away the old 'leggy' heather stems, but does not damage the roots, nor the peat in which they grow. New growth quickly springs up to feed the young grouse.

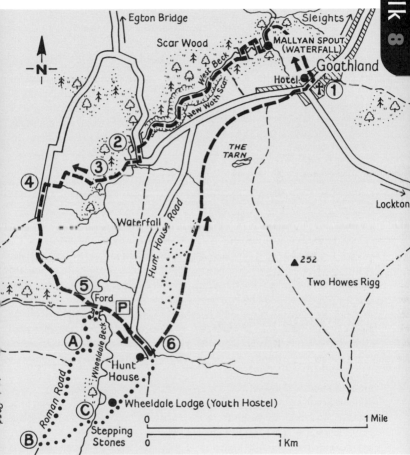

Walk 8 Directions

① Opposite the church go through the kissing gate beside the **Mallyan Spout Hotel**, signed 'Mallyan Spout'. Follow the path to a streamside signpost and turn left. Continue past the waterfall (take care after heavy rain). Follow the footpath signs, over two footbridges, over a stile and up steps, to ascend to a stile on to a road beside a bridge.

② Turn left along the road and climb the hill. Where the road bends left, go right along a bridleway through a gate. Turn left down a path to go over a bridge, then ahead between the buildings, through a gate and across the field.

Walk 8

③ Part-way across the field, go through a gate to the right into woodland. Ascend a stony track, go through a wooden gate to reach a facing gate as you leave the wood. Do not go through the gate, but turn right up the field, going left at the top through a gateway. Continue with a wall on your right and go through a waymarked gateway in the wall and up the field, to emerge through a gate on to a metalled lane.

WHAT TO LOOK FOR

In the valley of the West Beck, and especially near Mallyan Spout, you will see lots of **ferns**. Among the sorts you might spot are the male fern, with its pale green stems, the buckler fern, which has scales with a dark central stripe and paler edges, and the hartstongue fern, with its distinctive strap-like fronds. They are all typical of damp, humid areas, and like every fern, they are flowerless. Instead, they reproduce by means of spores – look under the leaves to find the characteristic dots that are the spore sacs or sporangia. The spores are dispersed by wind or by animals. Each young fern frond begins as a tight curl which gradually unfurls as it grows.

---

④ Turn left along the lane, go through a gate and follow the '**Roman Road**' sign. Go through another gate, still following the public bridleway signs as you join a green lane. Continue through a small handgate, to descend to another gate and then on until you reach a ford.

WHERE TO EAT AND DRINK

As you would expect from a popular village, there are cafés and snack bars dotted around Goathland, as well as ice cream vans on the green. The **Goathland Hotel** offers meals and bar snacks, and the restaurant at the **Mallyan Spout Hotel** has a fine reputation.

WHILE YOU'RE THERE

Take a trip on the **North Yorkshire Moors Railway**, which has a station in the valley below the village. Running from Pickering to Grosmont, the line was laid out by George Stephenson in 1836 for horse-drawn trains. It runs through spectacular Newtondale on its way north and ran steam trains from 1847 until it was closed in 1957. Fortunately, local enthusiasts preserved it, and it reopened in 1973. Most of its trains are steam-hauled.

---

⑤ Cross the ford and go straight ahead along the track, eventually to reach a road by farm buildings. Turn right up the road and, just before a wooden garage, turn left on a green track up the hillside.

⑥ Go straight ahead at a crossing track, passing a small cairn and bending left along the ridge. The obvious path is marked by a series of little cairns, eventually taking a left fork where the path divides, to go down a small gill and join a clear track. **Goathland church** soon comes into sight. Pass a bridleway sign and descend to the road near the church, to return to the start.

Wade's Causeway

If you have time, this extra loop takes you along part of Wade's Causeway.
See map and information panel for Walk 8

•**DISTANCE**•	6¼ miles (10km)
•**MINIMUM TIME**•	2hrs 30min
•**ASCENT / GRADIENT**•	613ft (187m) ▲▲▲
•**LEVEL OF DIFFICULTY**•	🚶🚶🚶

Walk 9 **Directions** (Walk 8 option)

At Point ⑤ on the main walk, cross the ford, then immediately turn right over a footbridge signed '**Roman Road**'. Go right at the end of the bridge and follow the path. Go over a stile and continue to the left, signed 'Roman Road'. Ascend to a wooden stile in the corner of the field and continue along the field-edge with a wall on your left. Go through a gate, and there is a signboard to the left with details of the Roman Road, Point Ⓐ.

Here you'll find out about the legend of Giant Wade and his wife Bell. He built the road to take his cattle to market, while she worked on Mulgrave Castle near Whitby. They had just one hammer, and they threw it the 18 miles (29km) between them as they needed it. They were a notoriously argumentative couple – the deep valley of the Hole of Horcum on the road between Whitby and Pickering is said to have caused by Wade scooping out a large handful of earth to throw at Bell. He missed, and the earth landed to form nearby Blakely Topping. Walk along the Roman Road and over a stile

beside a gate, following the line of the road. There is some dispute about whether this ¾ mile (1.2km) stretch of ancient causeway is in fact Roman, though that seems the most likely explanation. There is also argument about its surface – is what we see now its original condition, or are these merely the foundations, with the paving of the original Roman road having been removed by locals over the centuries? Whatever the reality, you can still make out the ditches at each side of the road, the culverts still covered by stone capping in places. The road took legionaries from Malton to the signal station near Whitby, but its route has not been authenticated all the way.

About ¼ mile (400m) beyond the gate look for a path leading off, left, down into the valley, Point Ⓑ. The path passes an anvil-shaped rock and descends steeply to stepping stones across the stream, Point Ⓒ. Go over a stile on the other side and continue along the grassy path. Do not go along the boardwalk but continue towards the building. The path passes the building and comes out on to a track. At the sign, continue straight ahead past another farm on to a metalled lane, then turn right at the garage and back to the main walk.

Walk 10

Staithes and the Scenic Coast

Staithes, where Captain Cook was apprenticed, Runswick Bay and Port Mulgrave are the highlights of this splendid coastal walk.

•DISTANCE•	5 miles (8km)
•MINIMUM TIME•	2hrs 30min
•ASCENT / GRADIENT•	436ft (130m) ▲▲▲
•LEVEL OF DIFFICULTY•	👫 👫 👫
•PATHS•	Field, woodland, coastal paths and tracks, 16 stiles
•LANDSCAPE•	Farmland, woodland and fine coastline
•SUGGESTED MAP•	aqua3 OS Outdoor Leisure 27 North York Moors – Eastern
•START / FINISH•	Grid reference: NZ 782185
•DOG FRIENDLINESS•	Dogs should be on leads, except in woodland
•PARKING•	Car park above village, signed off A174
•PUBLIC TOILETS•	Staithes

Walk 10 **Directions**

From the car park, walk past the garages and along a path by allotments. Turn right up the valley and follow the footpath signs through the houses, to meet the main road. Cross, go over a stile, through the field, then cross a track by two more stiles. Descend half right, go over a stile and cross the stream by the road bridge to the left, signed '**Hinderwell**'. After the bridge follow the waymark left, going over a stile and climbing steeply. Pass a gate with a stile beside it into woodland. This part

of the route is through the typical inland farming hinterland of the Yorkshire coast, with old native woodland lining the slopes of the streams that feed into Roxby Beck.

By the **Oakridge Nature Reserve** sign take the left fork, keeping along the ridge. At a field, go through the hedge and turn left along the field edge, turning left at a crossing path into the woods. Descend steps, cross a footbridge and go uphill over two stiles. Cross the field, then turn right after the gate and go along a track, which eventually bends left and becomes a metalled road through houses.

At the main road by a garage turn right, and then turn left along a path beside a bungalow. Go over a stile, through the field and over another stile on to a road. Turn right along the lane-side footpath to **Runswick Bay**. To see the view, go straight to the cliff top. The pretty village is at the foot of the steep

---

WHERE TO EAT AND DRINK ⓘ

Staithes has quite a number of eating places, as you'd expect from somewhere on the Captain Cook Trail. The **Cod and Lobster** near the harbour does meals and snacks, while two eating places with loyal and satisfied clientele are **Sea Drift**, which does splendid sandwiches, and the **Storehouse Bakery and Tea Shop**.

Walk 10

WHILE YOU'RE THERE ℹ️

West of Staithes is **Boulby Head**, the highest cliffs on the east coast, rising to 660ft (201m) Nearby is **Boulby potash mine**, the deepest in Europe. Its shafts descend 3,600ft (1,097m) and reach 5 miles (8km) out to sea. Morris Men have performed the world's deepest dance here and scientists use it to search for 'Dark Matter', said to make up 99 per cent of the universe.

cliffs, and has been there since at least the 13th century. In the 19th century the village briefly had a blast furnace, but is now renowned for its fine sandy beach.

The walk continues along the right side of the **Runswick Bay Hotel**. Go through a kissing gate and along the edge of a field to a stile to reach the coast. Turn left and walk along the **Cleveland Way** for a mile (1.6km) to go over a stile near **Port Mulgrave**, and then bend round the top of the valley to a kissing gate. From 1865 Port Mulgrave was an ironstone port. Its 3½ acre (1.4ha) harbour cost the Mulgrave Ironstone Company £45,000 to build. Trucks ran along a gantry above the pier and tipped their load into bunkers – there was a tunnel under the cliffs through which the railway line ran. The harbour remained in good condition until

1934, when the machinery was broken up and sold for scrap. During World War Two the breakwater was blown up so it couldn't be used by an invader.

Follow the coast road, which soon becomes a track. Go over a stile, along the coast, over a second stile and descend towards **Staithes**. Go over two stiles and into a fenced lane, which becomes a metalled lane by a farm. The path descends by a wall down into the village.

Clustered around the harbour and along the banks of the Roxby Beck, Staithes is one of the most attractive of the East Coast villages. Its narrow streets, lined with cottages, climb steeply up the hillside. Look out for the occasional wearer of the traditional white cotton Staithes bonnet, originally worn by the women to protect their heads as they carried baskets of mussels from the beach. It was in Staithes that young James Cook – the future Captain Cook – was apprenticed to William Sanderson's grocers' merchants in the main street. The Heritage Centre has a reconstruction of the street in his time.

To return to the car park, walk up the main street.

WHAT TO LOOK FOR ℹ️

Staithes harbour is protected by the shaley cliff of Cowbar Nab, and you are likely to see a number of small, colourfully-painted boats bobbing in the water or leaning in the mud if the tide is out. These are cobles (pronounced cobbles), the characteristic small fishing boats of the east coast. Inspired, it is said, by Viking boats, they are clinker-built – with the planks overlapping downwards – and are specially designed for launching from a beach. A guide of the 19th century said of the local men,

'During the winter and spring seasons they go out to sea in small flat bottomed boats, called Cobles, each carrying three men, and so constructed as to live in very tempestuous weather; in summer they go out in large boats, of from ten to twenty tons burden, called 'Five Men Cobles', they generally sail on Monday, and, if the weather permit, continue at sea the whole week.'

A Lastingham Round

From the ancient site of St Cedd's monastery to the attractive village of Hutton-le-Hole.

•DISTANCE•	4½ miles (7.2km)
•MINIMUM TIME•	2hrs
•ASCENT / GRADIENT•	463ft (141m) ▲▲▲
•LEVEL OF DIFFICULTY•	🚶🚶 🚶🚶 🚶
•PATHS•	Farm tracks and field paths, 8 stiles
•LANDSCAPE•	Moorland and woodland, with views
•SUGGESTED MAP•	aqua3 OS Outdoor Leisure 26 North York Moors – Western
•START / FINISH•	Grid reference: SE 729905
•DOG FRIENDLINESS•	Dogs should be on leads
•PARKING•	Village street in Lastingham. Alternative parking in car park at north end of Hutton-le-Hole
•PUBLIC TOILETS•	Hutton-le-Hole

BACKGROUND TO THE WALK

'In high and isolated hills, more fitted as a place of robbers and the haunt of wild animals than somewhere fit for men to live.'

So wrote the 8th-century historian Bede about Lastingham, which he had visited. This was where St Cedd, Bishop of the East Saxons and once a monk from Lindisfarne, founded his monastery in 654, and where he died in 664. Although nothing survives of his church, Lastingham remains a holy place, not least in the ancient and impressive crypt beneath the Norman church. This was built in 1078, when the monastery was refounded after destruction in Danish raids in the 9th century.

Court in Spaunton

Leaving Lastingham, the walk quickly reaches the single village street of Spaunton. Lined with cottages and farmhouses from the 17th century onwards, it seems typical of many villages on the North York Moors. But Spaunton has hidden secrets; the fields surrounding it are set out on a Roman pattern, and at the beginning of the 19th century a Roman burial was found near the village. Excavations, some 60 years later, also unearthed the foundations of a very large medieval hall, which indicated that Spaunton was once a large and important village, owned by St Mary's Abbey in York. When the estate was sold in the 16th century, the new landowners constituted a special court for the manor, grandly called the Court Leet and Court Baron with View of Frankpledge, which still meets to deal with the rights of those who can graze animals on the commons.

Hutton-le-Hole and the Quakers

Reckoned by many people to be one of the prettiest of North Yorkshire's villages, Hutton-le-Hole clusters around an irregular green and along the banks of the Hutton Beck. The village has an old Meeting House and a long association with the Society of Friends. One Quaker inhabitant, John Richard, was a friend of William Penn, founder of Pennsylvania. He spent much time preaching in America; it is said he rode more than 3,726 miles (6,000km) and acted as a mediator between the white settlers and the Native Americans. He finally retired to the village, where he died in 1753.

The Millennium Stone
Near the end of the walk you'll come across a new local landmark. Marking the year 2000, the people of Lastingham have placed a boulder carved with a cross on the hillside above the village. On it are two dates – AD 2000 and AD 654, the year in which St Cedd founded the original Lastingham monastery.

Walk 11

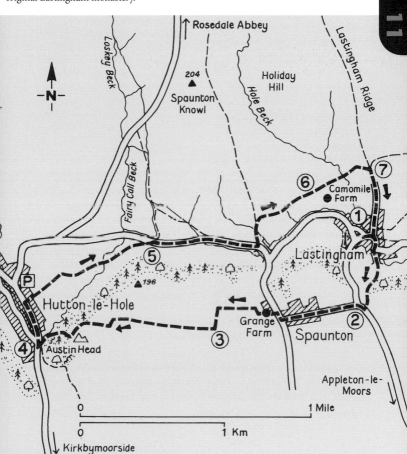

Walk 11 Directions

① Begin by **the Green** and follow signs to **Cropton**, **Pickering** and **Rosedale**, past the red telephone box. Where the road swings left, go right to wind over a small bridge and beside a stream. Ascend to a footpath sign, and go right, uphill, through a gate and through woodland to a handgate on to a road. Turn right, signed '**Spaunton**'.

② Follow the road through **Spaunton**, and bend right at the end of the village, then turn left by the public footpath sign over the

Walk 11

cattle grid into the farmyard. The waymarked track curves through the farm to reach another footpath sign, where the track bends left. At a barn the track bends left again.

③ After about 200yds (183m), follow a public footpath sign right and walk on to another sign as the track bends left. After 100yds (91m) take a footpath to the right, down the hill into woodland. Where the path divides, take the left fork down to a stile on your right, going off the track and down a steep grassy path into the valley. Descend beside a stream to a stile by a gate, which takes you on to the road in **Hutton-le-Hole**.

④ Turn right up the main street. Turn right at a yellow waymark by the **Beckside Gift Shop**. Go through a gate beside the **Barn Hotel** car park entrance and ahead through the garden and to the right of sheds to a stile. Go ahead over three stiles to a kissing gate before a footbridge. Follow the path through woodland to a gate and follow the grassy track to the road.

⑤ Turn right and follow the road for ½ mile (800m) and turn left at a footpath sign just before the road descends to a stone bridge. Follow the grassy path, going over a stile, to a footpath sign just before a farm.

WHAT TO LOOK FOR

There is a full range of activities at the **Ryedale Folk Museum** in Hutton-le-Hole, where old structures from around the North York Moors have been reconstructed as a hamlet. As well as an authentic Elizabethan manor house with a massive oak cruck frame, farm buildings, cottages and traditional long houses, you can see an early photographer's studio, a medieval glass kiln and a variety of agricultural tools and transport. There's also a fire engine and a hearse. Maypole dancing, rare breeds days and quilting are just some of the activities that take place during the year and you may catch the historic farm machinery working, or have the chance to try your hand at some of the almost-forgotten crafts.

⑥ Follow the direction indicated by the signpost to the left, bending alongside the wall beside a clump of trees and descending into a valley. Cross over the stream to a stile and a kissing gate. Continue walking with the wall on your right-hand side to another kissing gate and stile, which will lead you to a carved stone with a cross and a three-pointed sign.

⑦ Take none of the directions indicated by the sign, but turn right, downhill through a gate and on to the metalled road. Follow the road downhill back into the village of **Lastingham**.

WHILE YOU'RE THERE

If you're a real ale enthusiast, **Cropton Brewery**, 1½ miles (2.5km) east of Lastingham, is a place to head for. It can brew up to 60 barrels a week, and produces a range of beers with evocative names such as Monkmans Slaughter and Honey Gold, made with local honey. The Brewery and vsitor centre are open daily during the season, and by arrangement in the winter.

WHERE TO EAT AND DRINK

There is a range of cafés, tea rooms, restaurants and pubs in Hutton-le-Hole – the **Barn Hotel Tea Rooms** and the **Crown Hotel** are recommended. In Lastingham, the **Blacksmith's Arms** is a traditional village pub, while the excellent **Lastingham Grange** offers dinner and light lunches, as well as a full Sunday lunch, but is closed from mid-November to March.

Glorious Castle Howard

A walk around the well-ordered estates of one of the country's most famous stately homes.

Walk 12

•DISTANCE•	5¼ miles (8.4km)
•MINIMUM TIME•	2hrs
•ASCENT / GRADIENT•	256ft (68m) ▲▲▲
•LEVEL OF DIFFICULTY•	🚶🚶 🚶🚶 🚶🚶
•PATHS•	Field paths and estate roads, 1 stile
•LANDSCAPE•	Estate landscape and farmland
•SUGGESTED MAP•	aqua3 OS Explorer 300 Howardian Hills & Malton
•START / FINISH•	Grid reference: SE 708710
•DOG FRIENDLINESS•	Dogs should be on leads for much of walk
•PARKING•	Roadside car park near lake north west of Castle Howard, near crossroads
•PUBLIC TOILETS•	None on route (toilets at Castle Howard)

BACKGROUND TO THE WALK

One of the greatest of England's stately homes, Castle Howard was designed in 1699 by John Vanbrugh for Charles Howard, 3rd Earl of Carlisle. Vanbrugh was not an architect; he made his reputation first as a soldier, then as a playwright, so he was an odd choice. Nevertheless, he rose to the task in superb style. The north front, which we see from the first part of the walk, is hugely dramatic, with its giant columns, curving wings and crowning dome. One early visitor, Horace Walpole, wrote, 'I have seen gigantic palaces before, but never a sublime one.'

'A Perfect Landskip'

Everyone who visits Castle Howard will soon realise that this great house is set in a landscape that has been carefully manipulated as a setting for the house. The impressive 3¾ mile (6km) long, ruler-straight avenue that passes through the fortified Carrmire Gate and the Pyramid Gate, is only the start. Virtually everything of the estate you will see on the walk has been altered – hills rounded or levelled, rivers re-routed and dammed, lakes dug. All this was to create what the 18th-century writers called 'a perfect landskip', based on Italian paintings and dotted with classical buildings.

Pyramid and Mausoleum

There are three pyramids at Castle Howard – one of them is over the Pyramid Gate, one is in Pretty Wood and the third, the 'Great' Pyramid, is a landmark on the second part of this walk. Surrounded by four stone lanterns this pyramid (not open to the public) holds a monster bust of the 3rd Earl's great-great-grandfather. To the right as you approach the ornamental bridge over the New River, created around 1735, is the splendid Mausoleum, designed by Nicholas Hawksmoor. It is the final resting place for many generations of the Howard family, including Lord Howard of Henderskelfe, a former Chairman of the BBC. From the ornamental bridge there are fine views of the south façade of the house itself and its distinctive gilded dome.

Walk 12

Beyond the bridge is the Temple of the Four Winds, each portico inviting fresh breezes from the cardinal points of the compass. This little building by Vanbrugh is at the end of a terraced walk from the house. It is said that this walk was originally the main street of the village of Henderskelfe, swept away by the 3rd Earl and his architect in their grandiose scheme. Plans were drawn up for a new village nearby, but, somehow, it was never built. Beyond, notice the garden wall; the ground is higher on the house side, and is retained by a solid, rustic wall with a ditch in front of it – an early HaHa, which allowed uninterrupted views of the countryside without the inconvenience of sheep in the drawing room.

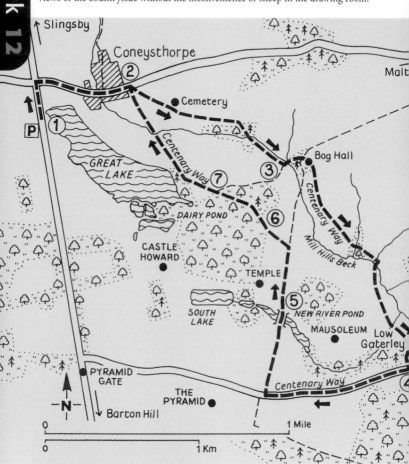

Walk 12 Directions

① From the car park, walk to the crossroads and turn right towards **Coneysthorpe**. Walk right through the village, and just beyond the 'Slow' sign go right through a tall white gate in a wall, following the **Centenary Way** sign.

② Go half left, crossing the track and head towards the further telegraph pole. Pass the cemetery on your left, walking now along a track. Through a gateway, go right along the edge of a field and, when you reach the double gate, turn right again along the edge of the wood. Continue along the track to reach a bridge.

Walk 12

③ Do not cross the bridge, but turn left along the track, following it as it bends right through the farm buildings, following the **Centenary Way** sign. The track passes through a wood, winds left over a bridge and then right. At the farm buildings follow the **Centenary Way** sign off to the right.

④ At the T-junction, turn right along the metalled lane. The **Pyramid** comes into view on your left-hand side. As you near the **Pyramid**, you will reach a staggered crossroads where the **Centenary Way** is signed to the left. Turn right here and descend to the bridge over the dammed stream, with the **Mausoleum** on the right and **Castle Howard** on the left.

⑤ Cross the bridge and continue up the track, with the **Temple of the Four Winds** on your left. The path goes over the ridge, then turns left to the park wall. Follow the wall as it bends left and go over a stile beside a white gate and continue along the track.

⑥ After about 30yds (27m), just beyond a gate on your left marked 'Private No Public Right of Way', go left off the gravel track down a grassy path. Follow this to another gravel track, where you turn left to reach a signpost. Turn right here and follow the track back to the tall white gate in **Coneysthorpe**. Turn left here, and retrace your route back to the car park.

WHILE YOU'RE THERE

You will certainly want to visit **Castle Howard** itself, with its marble-floored great hall, wonderful furniture and fine paintings, and to explore the grounds. This was where much of the television production of Evelyn Waugh's *Brideshead Revisited* was filmed. Younger visitors will enjoy the excitement of the challenging adventure playground.

WHAT TO LOOK FOR

Not everything at Castle Howard is 18th century. The largest piece of sculpture in the gardens is the grandiose Atlas fountain, with the Titan holding up the globe and surrounded by Tritons spouting water from their shells. This was put in place when the Victorian garden designer WE Nesfield laid out a new parterre at Castle Howard's south front. It was sculpted by Prince Albert's favourite artist John Thomas whose 'labours in this important and arduous undertaking have been unwearied, and his success has kept pace with his exertions,' as the Art Journal wrote in 1851. The Atlas Fountain came to Castle Howard after being on display at the Great Exhibition of that year.

Walk 13

The Iron Valley of Rosedale

Reminders of former industry are all around you on this route near Rosedale Abbey.

•DISTANCE•	3½ miles (5.7km)
•MINIMUM TIME•	1hr 30min
•ASCENT / GRADIENT•	558ft (170m) ▲▲ ▲▲
•LEVEL OF DIFFICULTY•	🏃 🏃 🏃
•PATHS•	Mostly field paths and tracks, 11 stiles
•LANDSCAPE•	Quiet valley and hillside farmland, with reminders of the iron industry
•SUGGESTED MAP•	aqua3 OS Outdoor Leisure 26 North York Moors – Western
•START / FINISH•	Grid reference: SE 708964
•DOG FRIENDLINESS•	Dogs should be on leads
•PARKING•	Roadside parking, with care, in Thorgill
•PUBLIC TOILETS•	None on route

BACKGROUND TO THE WALK

Rosedale is a quiet and peaceful valley that pushes north west into the heart of the North York Moors. The village of Rosedale Abbey gets its name from the former Cistercian nunnery of which only the angle of a wall remains. Yet little more than 100 years ago the village had a population ten times its present size. The reason was the discovery of ironstone in the hills in the mid 1850s. From 1856 onwards commercial exploitation began, new rows of cottages were built for the miners and, as one of the villagers wrote in 1869, 'The ground is hollow for many a mile underground… It's like a little city now but is a regular slaughter place. Both men and horses are getting killed and lamed every day.'

The East Mines

The dramatic remains of the Rosedale East Mines, which opened in 1865, can be seen during much of the walk. Now being cared for by the National Park Authority with help from English Heritage, they are a testament to the size of the mining operations. The long range of huge arches is the remains of the calcining kilns, where the ironstone was roasted to eliminate impurities and reduce its weight. They operated until 1879, when the owner, the Rosedale and Ferryhill Mining Company, collapsed, but resumed in 1881. The West Mines across the valley had stopped work by 1890, but the East Mines struggled on, burdened by rising costs, until the General Strike of 1926, which effectively killed them off.

The Iron Way

The mined iron ore from Rosedale was taken by rail from the mines and over the moorland to Ingleby, where it was lowered down the northern edge of the moors by tramway on the 1-in-5 gradient Ingleby Incline. The line had reached Rosedale in 1861, and the branch to the East Mines was opened in 1865. As many as 15 loaded wagons at a time were steam hauled round the top of Rosedale. The line closed in September 1928, and the last load was hauled down Ingleby Incline in June the following year. The track bed is now open for walkers to enjoy its engineered gradients.

The Vanished Chimney

For more than a century the village of Rosedale Abbey was dominated by an industrial chimney, more than 100ft (30m) tall. One of the steepest public roads in the country went past it to reach the heights of Spaunton Moor. The road is still there, but the chimney was demolished in 1972, a victim of the inability to raise the £6,000 needed to preserve it – and symptomatic of the public attitude to industrial archaeology that prevailed at the time.

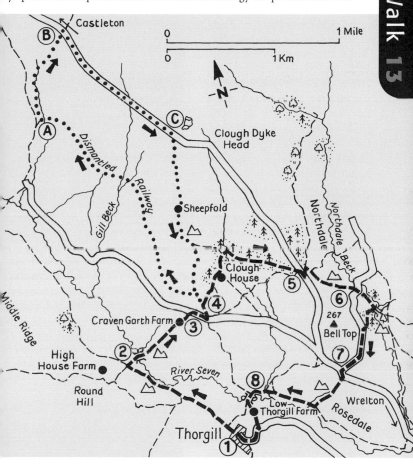

Walk 13 Directions

① From your parking place in the hamlet of **Thorgill**, continue up the lane, pass a public bridleway sign and go through a metal gate. Follow the track, going through a wooden gate and beginning to rise. Almost opposite a farmhouse on the left, go right over a wooden stile beside a gate.

② Walk down the slope to pass over the stream on a gated footbridge, then turn slightly left to go uphill on the opposite bank beside the trees. Continue through a gate into the field and walk ahead, going over a stile then through a metal gate into the yard of **Craven Garth Farm**. Go through another gateway and pass between the buildings to reach **Daleside Road**, a metalled country lane.

Walk 13

③ Turn right; just before reaching the cottage, turn left up a track by the parish notice board. A little way up the track look for a stile beside the gate to **Clough House**.

④ Go over the stile and follow the track downhill towards the wood, passing around the garden of **Clough House** and up to a stile, where you turn right and follow the waymarked path through the wood to reach a stile on to a road.

⑤ Turn right, then go left through a gate at a bridleway sign. Go down the grassy path to meet a level track. Turn left. Just before a gate, go right, following the bridleway sign. Continue downhill to reach a ladder stile, and go straight ahead across the field to reach a gateway on to a road by a bridleway sign.

⑥ Cross the road and continue ahead. After passing through a gateway, turn right at the footpath sign before the bridge. The track climbs steeply to a road. Turn left along the road to a T-junction.

⑦ Turn left. Opposite the **Bell End Farm** sign turn right through a gate, and continue down the field to a stile. The path bends and descends steeply. On reaching a fence, turn sharp right to go over a boardwalk and through a waymarked gate.

WHILE YOU'RE THERE ⓘ
Take the road north from Rosedale Abbey to Rosedale Head, where you will find **Young Ralph Cross**, symbol of the North York Moors National Park. A little way to the west is **Old Ralph**. Young Ralph is 18th century, replacing one on the site from at least 1200. It is said to have been put up by a farmer from Danby called Ralph who found a dead traveller on the spot. Old Ralph, on the highest part of Blakey Ridge, is possibly 11th century, and is said to be named after Auld Ralph of Rosedale, a herdsman employed by Guisborough Priory.

Follow the path over two stiles. Turn left down the track, which passes though a gateway, and go straight on.

⑧ Just beyond a gate, go left, following the stream, to cross a footbridge with stiles at each end. Follow the footpath uphill towards the farm buildings. Follow the waymarks through the buildings and up the farm track to reach a lane. Turn right and go back to the car parking place.

WHERE TO EAT AND DRINK ⓘ
The **Milburn Arms Hotel** in Rosedale Abbey offers high-class dining in its Priory Restaurant as well as meals in the beamed bar. The **Abbey Tea Rooms** provides coffee, light lunches and cream teas from Easter to the end of October.

WHAT TO LOOK FOR ⓘ
Looming over Thorgill at the start of the walk, and visible across the valley from most of the walk, is the bulk of **Blakey Rigg**, one of the most prominent of the Moors' heights, which divides Rosedale and Farndale. The Hutton-le-Hole to Castleton road follows the ridge's top for most of its length, and there are superb views from it. The Lion Inn is one of the most popular pubs in the area – and one of the most isolated. The Rigg is also known as a landmark on the Lyke Wake Walk across the Moors, celebrated in the *Lyke Wake Dirge* starting 'This aye night', set by Benjamin Britten. The walk follows the route that corpses were taken for burial. Those who believe in the existence of ley lines – those channels of mystical power that criss-cross the country – reckon that Blakey Rigg is the focus for several of them.

Along the Railway to Rosedale East Mines

Those who want to explore Rosedale's ironworking heritage further can take this loop, that starts by following the old railway line.
See map and information panel for Walk 13

•DISTANCE•	3½ miles (5.7km)
•MINIMUM TIME•	1hr 30min for this extra loop
•ASCENT / GRADIENT•	492ft (150m) ▲▲▲
•LEVEL OF DIFFICULTY•	🚶 🚶 🚶

Walk 14 Directions (Walk 13 option)

At Point ④ on the main walk don't go over the stile signed **Clough House**, but instead continue ahead up the lane. Go through a gate by the side of the farmhouse and continue up the track.

There is a National Park information board giving details of the railway route and the mines a little way along. Just beyond the information board, go through a wooden gate and follow the path ahead, to pass behind the ruined buildings. Turn right along the track of the old railway, which opened in 1865 and closed in 1928.

There are still reminders of the working days of the railway all the way along here, including a small platelayers' hut. Follow the old track bed for 1½ miles (2.4km). You will pass the remains of the **Rosedale East Mines** calcining kilns. Just after the track passes over a high embankment with woodland to the left, turn right uphill alongside a deep gill, Point Ⓐ.

After passing a wooden post, take the right hand fork to follow the line of posts. This marks the path that will eventually pass one of the many estate boundary markers of the moors and bring you to the metalled road by a public bridleway sign, Point Ⓑ.

Turn right and follow the minor road for about ¾ mile (1.2km) across the almost flat moorland plateau. Turn right again at the next bridleway sign (Point Ⓒ) by some old quarry workings and follow the path half left through the heather, passing to the right of another disused quarry, to reach the ruins of a sheepfold.

The track becomes more distinct now; follow it downhill towards the valley. When it bends to a wire fence, walk with the fence on your left to return to the gate by the National Park information board.

Turn left through the gate, and continue past the farm buildings and through a wooden gate. Then take the stile on the left beside the gate signposted to '**Clough House**'. You rejoin the main route back at Point ④ to complete the walk.

Princes and Poets at Sheriff Hutton

The ruined castle of the Nevilles provides the focus for this walk on the edge of the Vale of York.

•DISTANCE•	6 miles (9.7km)
•MINIMUM TIME•	2hrs 30min
•ASCENT / GRADIENT•	147ft (45m)
•LEVEL OF DIFFICULTY•	
•PATHS•	Field paths and tracks, a little road walking, 11 stiles
•LANDSCAPE•	Undulating farmland, with the castle set on a ridge
•SUGGESTED MAP•	aqua3 OS Explorer 300 Howardian Hills & Malton
•START / FINISH•	Grid reference: SE 654664
•DOG FRIENDLINESS•	Dogs should be kept on leads
•PARKING•	Roadside parking in village
•PUBLIC TOILETS•	Sheriff Hutton

Walk 15 Directions

From the crossroads – **The Square** – in the village centre, walk down the hill. Where the road bends right, turn left over a stile, signed '**Ebor Way**' and walk by a playground. Walk down the field, keeping the hedge on your right. You can clearly see **Sheriff Hutton Castle** to your left. Begun in 1382 by the Neville family, it originally had four huge corner towers, though only one remains to any great height. It was one of the power bases for the Earl of Warwick, known as the Kingmaker, whose daughter, Anne, married Richard III. Elizabeth of York, later queen to Henry VII, was imprisoned here until her future husband won the Battle of Bosworth in 1485. Sheriff Hutton Castle was subsequently owned by the Earl of Surrey, who employed the poet John Skelton to provide flattering verses for his household. Skelton's *Garlande of Laurell* was written here at Christmas in 1522.

Just past the cricket score box, go over a waymarked stile on your right, and continue along the cricket field edge. Go over another stile and straight on. At the end of the field, go over a plank bridge with stiles at each end. At the metalled track, turn left through the metal gate and continue through two more metal gates. Just after the third, by a pond on your left, go half right across the field, keeping left of the telegraph pole, to go over a stile in the crossing wire fence. In the top right hand corner, where the field narrows, go over a footbridge between two waymarked stiles. Turn left after the second and follow the

> **WHERE TO EAT AND DRINK** ⓘ
> The **Highwayman Inn** in The Square offers pub food and good beer. It has a beer garden and welcomes children. The **Castle Inn** has snack lunches on Saturday and full Sunday lunches.

Walk 15

hedge, veering slightly right to a footbridge and a gate in a crossing hedge. After the gate go half right across the field between humps in the ground. This is the remains of the deserted village of **East Lilling**. You can make out the rectangular platforms on which the houses were built, amidst the typical ridge and furrow of early ploughing.

Cross a stream and continue to a stile, and on in the same direction, to go over a boardwalk. After another gate with a bridge after it, bend right to go on to a road at a gate. Turn left, and left again at the crossroads, signed 'Bulmer'. About ¼ mile (400m) beyond **Thornton**

Grange Farm, go left up a signed track. Look south from the track to see York Minster in the distance. The skyline of York has been kept deliberately low to allow this huge building to make its full impact on the landscape.

Take the second turn right. Walk beside the farm buildings, and wind between to go through a metal gate, beside a pond and through another gate. Cross two fields to a gate in the crossing hedge. Continue towards the farm buildings, passing through another gate. Opposite the end of the farm buildings, turn left and follow the track to a stile beside a gate. Continue down the field towards the castle, going over a stile and footbridge to ascend the next field. Turn right, going left where the path divides and enter the churchyard through a gate. In the church, which was first built in the 11th century, is an alabaster figure that is said to be part of a monument to Edward, Prince of Wales, son of Richard III. He died at Middleham Castle in 1485 and his mother is supposed to have met his funeral procession here.

Leave the churchyard by another gate on to the road and turn left back to **The Square**.

Walk

16

Remote Cockayne and Rudland Rigg

A walk in Bransdale from the remote hamlet of Cockayne and along an ancient moorland track.

•DISTANCE•	4 miles (6.4km)
•MINIMUM TIME•	2hrs
•ASCENT / GRADIENT•	754ft (230m) ▲▲▲
•LEVEL OF DIFFICULTY•	🚶🚶 🚶🚶 🚶🚶
•PATHS•	Field paths and moorland tracks, a little road walking, 1 stile
•LANDSCAPE•	Farmland and heather moorland
•SUGGESTED MAP•	aqua3 OS Outdoor Leisure 26 North York Moors – Western
•START / FINISH•	Grid reference: SE 620985
•DOG FRIENDLINESS•	On leads in farmland
•PARKING•	Roadside parking near cattle grid at T-junction in Cockayne
•PUBLIC TOILETS•	None on route

BACKGROUND TO THE WALK

The hamlet of Cockayne is tucked away at the end of Bransdale, one of the most remote of the valleys of the North York Moors. Here the road loops back into the lower moors, and walking country lies ahead. Its remoteness may be the origin of its name; the 'Land of Cockayne' was a distant and mythical place, of idleness and luxury, popular in medieval literature. Pleasant though Cockayne may be in good weather, any idleness in winter is no doubt enforced by the results of its isolation.

The Literary Mill

After leaving Cockayne, the first substantial building you will come to is Bransdale Mill. Here the infant Hodge Beck has been dammed into a series of pools to feed the millwheel. They may date back as far as the 13th century, when Bransdale Mill is first recorded. The current buildings are, however, from 600 years later, when the mill was rebuilt, as the inscription says, by local landowner William Strickland. His son Emmanuel was responsible for the inscriptions that adorn the buildings, in Latin, Greek and Hebrew. Emmanuel was vicar of Ingleby Greenhow, 6¼ miles (10km) to the north, over the hills.

Making Tracks

After the climb from the traditional farm buildings at Spout House, the walk takes you on some of the many tracks that cross the high moorland. As you pass the grouse butts you are on an ancient route that traverses the ridge from Farndale (famous for its wild daffodils) into Bransdale. Soon you will turn left along Westside Road. Like most of the main routes in the North York Moors, it follows the summit of the ridge; this one is Rudland Rigg. Westside Road is one of the longest (and straightest) in the National Park, running 34¼ miles (55km) north from Kirkbymoorside to leave the northern edge of the Moors near Kildale. Along its route you will find old stone waymarks and boundary stones. As you leave the track along the ridge, you are rewarded with a view back down into Bransdale.

Acorns Restore

Much of the north end of the valley is owned by the National Trust, and Bransdale Mill, passed at the beginning of the walk, is a centre for volunteers on the Trust's Acorn Projects – indeed, it was they who restored the buildings. Bransdale has also been suggested as the home of Robin Hood (fairly handy for his Bay, perhaps!), but this is probably only the result of confusion with Barnsdale Forest, more than 31½ miles (50km) to the south, which is a rather more likely area for the outlaw's home.

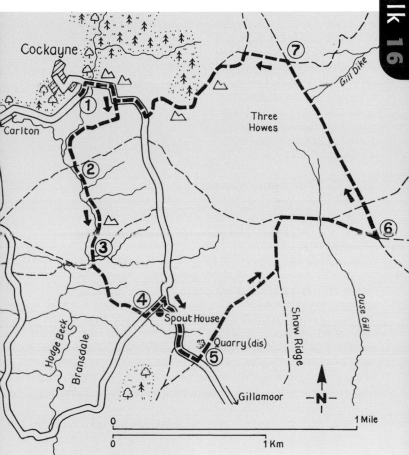

Walk 16 Directions

① Cross the cattle grid and turn right at the T-junction towards **Kirkbymoorside**. Follow the road uphill and, as it bends sharp left, go through a gate signed '**Bransdale Base Camp**' and follow the track down the hill to a gate. Continue along the track.

② At the signpost by the crossroads of tracks next to **Bransdale Mill** carry straight on, continuing parallel with the stream on your right. Go through two gates, following the side of the stream. Climb over a slight ridge to reach another gate. Continue with a wire fence on your right, keeping on top of the ridge, then descend to a waymarked gate.

Walk 16

③ Cross the stream and continue ahead. At the top of a rise go half left across the field, making for a corner of the wall. Go through three field gates and follow the grassy track along the field edge to another waymarked gate. At the top of the field go over a stile beside a wooden gate on to a lane.

④ Turn left. Pass the farm buildings to a road junction and turn right. Follow the road uphill for ¼ mile (400m), passing a bend sign. Where a track joins the road from the right, turn left on to the moorland.

⑤ The path through the heather is indistinct, but goes half right, passing a quarried area. You will eventually reach a track, where you turn left. Follow the track to reach a metal barrier. Turn right at the junction just beyond and follow the track to a crossroads.

⑥ Turn left and follow the gravel track for ¾ mile (1.2km), past a boundary stone and three howes. Where the gravel track is crossed by a grass track, turn left.

⑦ Follow the track downhill. It passes the end of a wood and continues to wind downhill. Go through a wooden gate and then bend left to another gate on to the lane. Turn right and follow the road back to the starting point.

Hidden York

Through streets and alleys of the historic walled city.

•DISTANCE•	3¼ miles (5.2km)
•MINIMUM TIME•	1hr 30min
•ASCENT / GRADIENT•	82ft (25m)
•LEVEL OF DIFFICULTY•	
•PATHS•	City pavements
•LANDSCAPE•	Historic city
•SUGGESTED MAP•	AA York streetplan
•START / FINISH•	Grid reference: SE 598523
•DOG FRIENDLINESS•	City streets, so dogs on leads
•PARKING•	Marygate Car Park, off Bootham
•PUBLIC TOILETS•	Parliament Street and Museum Gardens

BACKGROUND TO THE WALK

St Olave's Church, at the start of the walk, was founded in 1055 by Siward, Earl of Northumbria and heavily repaired after it was used as a gun platform in the Civil War Siege of York. Further along, past the library, look right as you ascend the steps, to the Anglian Tower. Built on the Roman ramparts during the time the Anglians ruled York (from the 6th century), this small building is now surrounded by the exposed layers of successive York defensive walls.

Abbot and Archbishop

The King's Manor, on your left as you go towards Exhibition Square, was the house of the Abbot of St Mary's, and was appropriated by the King in 1539. The residence of the President of the Council of the North from 1561 to 1641, it was apartments until 1833 and then a school. Since 1963 it has been leased to York University. The Minster Library, approached through Dean's Park, north of the Minster, is the only remaining substantial part of the palace of the Archbishops of York. Built about 1230 as the palace's chapel, it became the library in the 19th century.

Vicars and Nonconformists

Bedern, off Goodramgate, was where the Vicars Choral of the Minster lived. They sang the Minster services, and had their own Chapel and Hall (both of which you will pass) as well as a wooden walkway to the Minster precincts to avoid the undesirables who inhabited the area. On St Saviourgate is the red-brick Unitarian Chapel. Designed in the shape of an equal-armed cross with a little tower, it was built for the Presbyterians in 1692. Lady Peckitt's Yard goes by the spectacular half-timbered Herbert House of about 1620. As you turn into Fossgate, notice Macdonald's furniture shop opposite. This was the Electric Theatre, York's first cinema, built in 1911. After passing Clifford's Tower and reaching Castlegate, visit Fairfax House, a fine town house of the 1740s with its interiors beautifully restored in the 1980s after it, too, was used as a cinema for many years. On King's Staith, once the main wharf for the city, is the 17th-century King's Arms Inn, which has the distinction of being Britain's most flooded pub. Ouse Bridge was for centuries the only crossing place linking the

Walk 17

two banks of the river. This 19th-century bridge replaced two earlier ones: the Elizabethan bridge had houses on it. Holy Trinity Church off Goodramgate has delightful box pews and uneven floors. On the way back to Marygate, notice the round St Mary's Tower at its junction with Bootham. Part of the walls of St Mary's Abbey, it was blown up in 1644 during the Civil War and later rebuilt, rather inaccurately.

Walk 17 Directions

① Walk back into **Marygate**, turn left, cross the road and enter **Museum Gardens** through the archway. Follow the path straight ahead, passing the Observatory, and leave the gardens by the lodge.

② Turn left, then left again towards the library. Go left through a gate, and along the side of the library.

Go up the steps, and through a gate in the wall. At the bottom of the slope, turn right and follow **Abbey Wall** into **Exhibition Square**.

③ Cross at the traffic lights and go through **Bootham Bar**. A few yards on your left, take a passageway beside the Hole in the Wall pub and turn right down **Precentor's Court**. By the **Minster** go left through the gate, signed 'York Minster Library and Archives'.

Walk 17

④ Follow the path left to the Minster Library building. Bend right through the gate and along the cobbled road. Turn left by the postbox down **Chapter House Street,** bending right into **Ogleforth**. At the crossroads turn right, then go left through an archway opposite the National Trust tea rooms.

⑤ Bear right into **Bartle Garth,** which bends left. At the T-junction turn right, and then go left down **Spen Lane**. Opposite Hilary House go right along **St Saviourgate**. At the T-junction turn left to the crossroads, then right. Next to Jones's shoe shop on the left take a passage, **Lady Peckitt's Yard**.

⑥ Go under the building then turn left to **Fossgate**. Turn right, go over the bridge and then turn right along **Merchantgate**. At the T-junction, cross the road and take the glazed passageway beside the bridge, signed '**Jorvik Viking Centre**', into the car park by **Clifford's Tower**.

⑦ Bend right and go to the right of the Hilton Hotel. Just before the Job Centre, go left down **Friargate**, right along **Clifford Street**, and left by York Dungeon. At the riverside turn right, ascend the steps by **Ouse Bridge** and turn right. At the traffic lights turn left by **St Michael's Church**. By the NatWest Bank go right, forking left by The Link shop.

⑧ Go ahead to cross **Parliament Street** and pass **St Sampson's Church**. Go straight on at the next crossroads into **Goodramgate**. Opposite Bon Marche go through a gateway into Holy Trinity churchyard, and leave by a passage to your left, to reach **Low Petergate**. Turn right then take the next left into **Grape Lane**. Where it bends left, turn right down the narrow **Coffee Yard** into **Stonegate**.

⑨ Go left to **St Helen's Square** and turn left by the TSB. Go straight on at the next crossroads back to **Exhibition Square**. At the traffic lights turn left up **Bootham**. Turn left down **Marygate** by the circular tower to return to the car park.

WHAT TO LOOK FOR

You should visit **York Minster**. Allow time to visit The Foundations while you are there. It's worth the admission fee to walk through the building's history, including Roman walls, some with painted plaster intact, and medieval foundations. Also visit The Treasury and the shrine of St William of York.

WHILE YOU'RE THERE

In the Roman and medieval city, the Greek-temple style of the **Yorkshire Museum** in Museum Gardens, designed in 1827, is an incongruous sight. Indeed, the Victorian Gothic architect Pugin called it a 'detestable building'; 'it would have been hardly possible,' he wrote, 'to have erected more offensive objects than these buildings in the immediate vicinity of one of the purest specimens of Christian architecture in the country.' Among its excellent displays are Roman objects, sculpture from St Mary's Abbey, Viking remains and the medieval Middleham Jewel of finely-engraved gold.

Walk 18

Roseberry Topping and Captain Cook Country

An ascent of Roseberry Topping for fine views and reminders of one of Britain's great explorers.

•DISTANCE•	5½ miles (9km)
•MINIMUM TIME•	2hrs 30min
•ASCENT / GRADIENT•	1,214ft (370m) ▲▲▲
•LEVEL OF DIFFICULTY•	🚶🚶 🚶🚶 🚶🚶
•PATHS•	Hillside climb, then tracks and field paths, 3 stiles
•LANDSCAPE•	One of the best 360-degree views in Yorkshire
•SUGGESTED MAP•	aqua3 OS Outdoor Leisure 26 North York Moors – Western
•START / FINISH•	Grid reference: NZ 570128
•DOG FRIENDLINESS•	Off leads, except in farmland
•PARKING•	Car park on A173 just south of Newton under Roseberry
•PUBLIC TOILETS•	In car park at foot of Roseberry Topping

BACKGROUND TO THE WALK

Visible for miles around and one of the most distinctive of all English hills, Roseberry Topping, 1,051ft (320m) high, was once an integral part of the North York Moors plateau. Over the millennia, however, the forces of nature eroded the land around it, but the Topping itself was protected by a cap of harder sandstone. In time it became an isolated conical hill, stranded above the plain of the River Tees. Through the centuries it has been called many things, from Odinburgh (after the Norse God) to Rosemary Torp (by the notoriously inaccurate Daniel Defoe). Roseberry means 'fortress in the heath' and Topping, a 'point' – though there is no sign of a fortress there now.

Iron at Fault

Roseberry Topping retained its conical perfection until the night of 8th August 1912, when a huge chunk of land fell from its south west slope and gave it the now-characteristic jagged profile. The immediate cause of the fall was the ironstone mining operations that had been burrowing into the slopes of the hill, since 1880, when the Roseberry Ironstone Company opened its first seam. Like much of this part of the North York Moors, Roseberry Topping is rich in ironstone, and it seemed a prize worth winning. The company survived for only three years, but the seam was later re-opened first by the Tees Furnace Company and then by its successor Burton and Sons. Burton's were blamed for the 1912 collapse, and for another landslide ten years later, but the topping is geologically unstable and could have slipped at any time.

Cook's Tours

After the descent from Roseberry Topping, and the climb again to the woodland, the track descends over Great Ayton Moor. Ahead, the Captain Cook Monument, a stone obelisk 51ft (15.5m) high, dominates the view. The great explorer was born in 1728 within sight of Roseberry Topping at Marton (then a village, but now a suburb of Middlesbrough) and went to school at nearby Great Ayton. The monument was erected in 1827, with an inscription that names James Cook as 'amongst the most celebrated and most admired benefactors of the human race.' From 1736 his father worked at Aireyholme Farm (not open to the public), near Point ⑥ on the walk.

Mine Houses
Just after you have gone through the gate after Point ⑤, the dips and hollows in the ground to the left are the remains of another ironstone mine, Ayton Banks. This was last worked in the 1920s. A little further on, you will pass Gribdale Terrace, a typical row of cottages built to house the iron miners and their families.

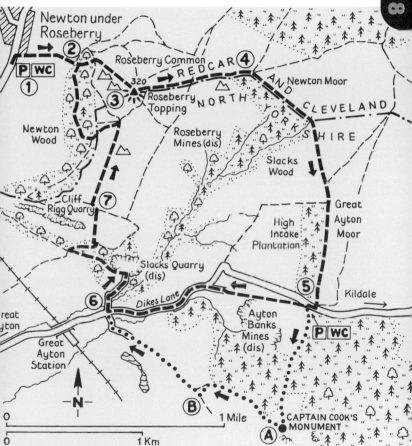

Walk 18 Directions

① Take the rough lane beside the car park towards **Roseberry Topping**. The path goes through a gateway then rises to a second gate at the beginning of the woodland.

② Go through the gate into National Trust Land and turn left. There is a well-worn path to the summit, with several variations to the route. Some are easier than others but whichever you take, it is a stiff climb to the trig point on the top of the hill.

Walk 18

③ From the summit, take the **Cleveland Way** path on the opposite side from the ascent, going down a track which rises through a gate to the corner of woodland. Go through another gate and turn right alongside the wood.

④ Follow this track as it follows the edge of the wood. It passes through another gate and goes past a second area of wood, descending the hillside to reach a road.

WHILE YOU'RE THERE ⓘ

Roseberry Topping attracts more than 100,000 visitors each year, many of whom make it to the summit. As a result, it is in constant danger from erosion, both from those thousands of feet and from the sometimes severe weather that can affect the northern slope of the Moors. The National Trust, which owns it, needs to maintain a balance between access and conservation. You may find, therefore, that some parts are cordoned off, and access is limited to other areas. Stone and soil – in the last campaign more than 200 tonnes – are imported to try to stabilise the paths. Visitors can help by making sure that they stay on the tracks and by obeying any warning signs.

---

⑤ Turn right, cross the cattle grid and bear left past a bench to a gate. Turn right to go over a stile, down the field, over another stile and out into a lane. Walk past the cottages to reach a road, where you go straight ahead.

⑥ At a crossroads go right, down **Aireyholme Lane**. Follow the lane as it winds past houses, then take a

---

WHERE TO EAT AND DRINK ⓘ

There is often a **refreshment caravan** in the car park at the foot of Roseberry Topping, and an **ice cream van** up the lane. Otherwise, head for nearby Newton under Roseberry, where the **King's Arms** is recommended by locals for its atmosphere, and its meals – especially the puddings.

---

signed footpath left through woodland. After ½ mile (800m), go right up a path ascending through the woods, turning left at a crossing path and continuing along the edge of the woodland. Continue bearing right to reach a track to farm buildings which goes left then right, to a gate.

⑦ Walk across two fields to a stile, then continue uphill to the tower. Beyond it, take a grassy path left down a gully, to a gate into woodland. Follow the path downhill through the woods to return to the gate at the top of the lane leading back to the car park.

Roseberry Topping – A Longer Walk

To get another perspective on Roseberry Topping, and to see the Monument to Captain Cook, take this extra loop.
See map and information panel for Walk 18

•DISTANCE•	7 miles (11.3km)
•MINIMUM TIME•	3hrs 15min
•ASCENT / GRADIENT•	1,640ft (500m) ▲▲▲
•LEVEL OF DIFFICULTY•	🚶 🚶 🚶

Walk 19 Directions (Walk 18 option)

From Point ⑤ on the main walk, turn right, up the track into **Gribdale Forest**, following the **Cleveland Way** sign. Follow the path for ½ mile (800m) to reach the **Captain Cook Monument**, Point Ⓐ. There was national sorrow when Cook was killed in Hawaii in 1779, but it took another 49 years for this monument to be erected. He is described in the inscription as 'a man of nautical knowledge inferior to none, in zeal, prudence and energy superior to most.' It tells us he will be remembered 'while the art of navigation shall be cultivated… the spirit of enterprise, commerce and philanthropy shall animate the sons of Britain, [and] while it shall be deemed a Christian Nation to spread civilisation and the blessings of the Christian faith among pagan and savage tribes.' The monument has lasted longer than the North Eastern Daily Gazette, whose readers subscribed in 1895 for its restoration. With superb views all around, it is a fitting monument to Cook –

especially as his birthplace in Marton has long been demolished and his family's Great Ayton home was moved to Australia in 1934.

With your back to the inscription on the monument, walk half right along a path that passes through two standing stones. Go left, following the waymark where the path divides, and left again where the path forks. The path goes steeply down through the wood to reach a green track, Point Ⓑ. Turn right then, after 200yds (183m), go left at a crossing. Walk down to a gate and continue downhill with a wall to your right, bending right on a track down towards a lake. Continue through a gateway and along the footpath, which soon becomes a track then a metalled lane, to a crossroads at Point ⑥ on the main walk.

WHAT TO LOOK FOR ⓘ
Visit **Great Ayton**, where you can see the schoolroom where Captain Cook studied between 1736 and 1741, and a rather mawkish statue of him as a boy on the attractive village green. Great Ayton has always been a strongly Quaker village, though the independent school they founded in 1824 has closed.

Walk 20

Vikings and a Cardinal Beside the Ouse

From Wistow to Cawood, and a return along the riverbank, with reminders of 1066 and Cardinal Wolsey.

•DISTANCE•	7 miles (11.3km)
•MINIMUM TIME•	3hrs
•ASCENT / GRADIENT•	Negligible
•LEVEL OF DIFFICULTY•	
•PATHS•	Field paths and tracks, and river embankment, 8 stiles
•LANDSCAPE•	Flat farmland and river flood plain
•SUGGESTED MAP•	aqua3 OS Explorer 290 York, Selby & Tadcaster
•START / FINISH•	Grid reference: SE 593356
•DOG FRIENDLINESS•	Dogs should be on leads at all times
•PARKING•	Roadside parking in Wistow village
•PUBLIC TOILETS•	None on route

Walk 20 Directions

Start by the door of **Wistow church** and walk past the **Black Swan**. At the road junction beyond, turn left along **Station Road**. At the next junction turn right. Where the road bends left, go straight ahead up a track by a footpath sign. Where the track divides go right and follow the hedgerow round to the right. Ahead of you is the tall, oddly-shaped tower of **Wistow Mine**. Wistow is in the Selby Coal Field, and the pit-head buildings reflect modern mining design.

The path then goes half left across the field to the end of a hedge and crosses a ditch. Go straight ahead with the ditch on your right and at the next hedge go ahead, following the wire fence as it curves to follow the ditch. Pass through a gateway in a fence and continue through the field to a gap in the top right-hand corner. Cross a ditch and follow the

path as it winds towards a double telegraph pole, and on through a gate to join a track beside glasshouses, towards a brick house and then on to a lane. This is fertile farming country, on the rich flood plain of the River Ouse. A wide variety of crops is grown, including sugar beet, which you may see later being transported by barge along the river.

Turn right, then go left beyond the house, up the field side to cross a footbridge. Turn right and walk across the field. Cross the ditch and continue towards the right of the red-roofed houses to reach a track by allotments. Follow the track to

---

WHERE TO EAT AND DRINK

The **Black Swan** in Wistow has decent beer but no meals, while **Il Giardino** Italian restaurant opens only in the evenings. In Cawood the **Ferry Inn**, which has been voted Pub of the Year several times by the local newspaper, offers home-cooked food and real ale.

Walk 20

> ### WHILE YOU'RE THERE ℹ
> Look in **Cawood church** as you pass. It is set at the highest point of the village (even though it is very close to the river). It dates from around 1150 – but it was first mentioned only in 1294. It probably served as the castle's chapel until its own was built in around 1270. Inside is a monument to Archbishop Mountain, a local man, successively Bishop of Lincoln and London before becoming Archbishop of York. He survived his enthronement by only a fortnight. There is also a plaque to a choirboy who became an air-ship steward and died in the R101 disaster.

meet a crossing hedge, and turn left down the field edge. Go right by the fence and cross a stile beside a footpath sign into a sports field. Leave by a wooden stile beyond the slide, to emerge, by another stile, on to the road. Turn right up the road, turning left at the junction, towards Tadcaster. Follow the road past the gatehouse to **Cawood Castle**.

This is all that remains of the former seat of the Archbishops of York, on a site given to them by King Athelstan around 930. The gatehouse is 15th century, and is now let for holidays by the Landmark Trust. Cawood was home to Cardinal Wolsey, and it was here that he was arrested for treason

against King Henry VIII. It was the nearest he ever got to York, even though he was its archbishop.

At the traffic lights turn right and, just before the bridge, go right again, down **Old Road**. Where the road bends right continue ahead down **Water Row** to the gate into the churchyard. Pass to the left of the church to walk along the river bank, going over five stiles. As the river bends southwards you are opposite **Riccall Landing**. This is where the Norwegian fleet of Harald Hardrada landed in 1066, in its attempt to defeat King Harold Godwinson. Three hundred fearsome Viking ships were sailed or rowed up the Ouse, and after the troops disembarked they marched to Stamford Bridge where, though superior in numbers, they were defeated by the English army. Of the 300 ships, only two dozen sailed back to Norway.

Beyond a brick building with a footbridge to it, turn right at a crossing track, passing a pond. Turn left at the T-junction and follow the road to another T-junction. Turn right and follow the road back into the village, bearing left past the school and then right by the 'no through road' sign to take you back to the church.

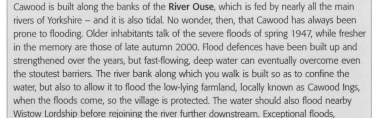

> ### WHAT TO LOOK FOR ℹ
> Cawood is built along the banks of the **River Ouse**, which is fed by nearly all the main rivers of Yorkshire – and it is also tidal. No wonder, then, that Cawood has always been prone to flooding. Older inhabitants talk of the severe floods of spring 1947, while fresher in the memory are those of late autumn 2000. Flood defences have been built up and strengthened over the years, but fast-flowing, deep water can eventually overcome even the stoutest barriers. The river bank along which you walk is built so as to confine the water, but also to allow it to flood the low-lying farmland, locally known as Cawood Ings, when the floods come, so the village is protected. The water should also flood nearby Wistow Lordship before rejoining the river further downstream. Exceptional floods, though, make these defences vulnerable, even when they are reinforced with sandbags, and homes are still prone to flooding, even at some distance from the river.

Monks and an Astronomer at Byland Abbey

From the romantic ruins of Byland Abbey to an old observatory – and back through the fish pond.

•DISTANCE•	5 miles (8km)
•MINIMUM TIME•	2hrs 30min
•ASCENT / GRADIENT•	623ft (190m) ▲ ▲ ▲
•LEVEL OF DIFFICULTY•	👫 👫 👫
•PATHS•	Woodland tracks, field paths, 11 stiles
•LANDSCAPE•	Undulating pasture and woodland on slopes of Hambleton Hills
•SUGGESTED MAP•	aqua3 OS Outdoor Leisure 26 North York Moors – Western
•START / FINISH•	Grid reference: SE 548789
•DOG FRIENDLINESS•	Dogs can be off lead in woodland where indicated
•PARKING•	Signed car park behind Abbey Inn in Byland
•PUBLIC TOILETS•	At Byland Abbey

BACKGROUND TO THE WALK

In 1134 a party of Savigniac monks set out from their English mother house in Furness on the west coast of Cumbria to found a new monastery. Forty-three years and six moves later, Byland was founded as their permanent home, and by then they had become part of the Cistercian Order. The final move was from nearby Stocking, where they had settled in 1147. The relocation to Byland in 1177 must have been long planned, for Byland's earliest buildings, the lay brothers' quarters, were complete by 1165; everything had to be in order for the arrival of the monks themselves.

The Abbey Buildings

The most impressive parts of the ruins remaining today are in the church – and especially the remnants of the fine rose window in the west front. Beneath it the main door leads into the nave, the lay brothers' portion of the church. The monks used the east end. Although the walls of the south transept collapsed in 1822, that area of the church still retains one of Byland's greatest treasures – the geometrically tiled floors, with their delicate patterns in red, cream and black.

Work and Pray

The monks at Byland Abbey, like all of their Cistercian brethren, rose at about 2AM for the first service, Vigil. Two more services and a meeting followed before they dined at midday. They spent the afternoon working at their allotted tasks, and there were three more services, after which they went to bed, at around 8:30PM. The choir monks did some of the manual work in the abbey and on its estate, but the Cistercians also had lay brothers to work for them. They, too, took vows (though simpler ones) and had their own church services. The Black Death in the 14th century, which radically changed the supply of agricultural labour, effectively ended the tradition of lay brothers in English monasteries.

Oldstead Observatory

At the highest point of the walk is Oldstead Observatory, built on the splendidly-named Mount Snever by John Wormald, who lived at Oldstead Hall in the valley below. It was a celebration, as the rather worn inscription tells us, of Queen Victoria's accession to the throne. At just over 40ft (12 m) high, 1,146ft (399m) above sea level, it is high enough to scan the heavens, though history does not record if Mr Wormald made any startling astronomical discoveries through his roof-mounted telescope.

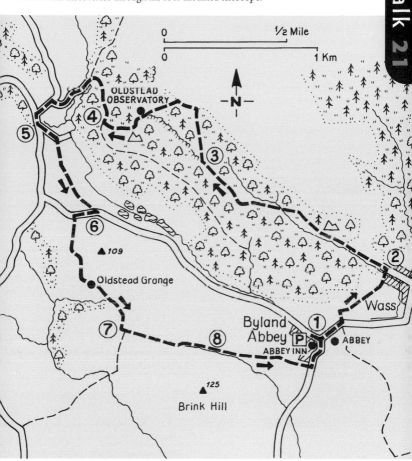

① From the car park, walk towards the abbey ruins, then turn left along the abbey's north side. At a public footpath sign, go left through a gateway, and right through a waymarked gate just before the second set of gateposts. After a second gateway bear half left to a waymarked gate behind a bench. Go through two more gates and on to a metalled lane.

② Turn left. At the top of the lane go through a gate signed 'Cam Farm, Observatory'. The path climbs then leaves the wood edge to rise to a terrace. After a stile take the left-hand path, following **Cam Farm**. Where three paths meet, turn

Walk 21

right, climbing uphill on a track which levels out to reach a large open space.

③ Turn right and, just before a waymarked metal gate, turn left along the wood edge. Follow the path to **Oldstead Observatory**. Pass to the left of the Observatory and go down a slope to a track running steeply downhill to a signpost.

④ Turn right, signed '**Oldstead**'. Follow the track as it curves left to become a metalled lane. Turn left at the T-junction, and left again on to the road by a seat. Just before the road narrows sign, turn left.

> **WHAT TO LOOK FOR** ℹ️
> The lumps and bumps of the final field you cross on the walk are the remains of the **monks' ponds**. It is difficult to visualise the abbey in the Middle Ages almost surrounded by water. There was a large pond that stretched almost ½ mile (800m) from east to west, to the north of the abbey buildings, which was used to flush the drains, and two more south and south east. To the south west, where this walk passes through, was a roughly triangular pond, bounded by a bank supporting the abbey's mill. The ponds were also used for breeding fish, one of the most important staples of the monks' diet. They practiced large-scale fish farming at nearby Oldstead Grange.

⑤ Go through some gateposts and over a cattle grid. Then, as the avenue of trees ends, take a waymarked footpath to the right, uphill. Climb up to a stile, bending around to the left beside the woodland to another stile, marked by a fingerpost. Continue past another waymarker and over a waymarked stile. The footpath goes between a hedge and a wire fence, then over another stile on to a metalled road.

> **WHERE TO EAT AND DRINK** ℹ️
> There are two country inns with good food on the walk. The **Abbey Inn** in Byland, directly opposite the Abbey, has old beams and flagged floors, and offers sandwiches and meals at lunchtime, and fine dinners. The **Wombwell Arms** at Wass has bistro-style food, with sandwiches and ploughman's at lunchtime. Both serve good traditional Yorkshire beers.

⑥ Turn right then, just beyond the road sign which indicates a bend, take a track to the left by the **Oldstead Grange** sign. As you near the house, turn left towards some barns and wind your way through the farmyard to a stile by a metal gate. Bear right downhill on the track, then bend slightly right to a waymarked stile.

⑦ Over the stile turn left and go through the wood to a **Byland Abbey** signpost. Follow the path as it bends left by another sign, go over a stile and down the field with the hedge on your left to another signpost. Go over a stile beside a metal gate and along the field with a hedge on your right.

⑧ Go over two stiles then bear slightly left to another stile. Go half left to a signpost in the hedge by a metal gate. Follow the fence, then on to the road by a wooden stile. Turn left, then left again past the **Abbey Inn** to the car park.

> **WHILE YOU'RE THERE** ℹ️
> Take a trip to nearby Kilburn to visit the **Mouseman Visitor Centre**. Here Robert Thompson, born in 1876, worked at his now-famous furniture, each piece carved with his characteristic mouse. Oak furniture is still made by his successors, and the centre demonstrates the history of the firm and its work.

A Whirl Around Whorlton and Swainby

From the once-industrial village of Swainby, a walk with fine views from the Moors and a taste of history in Whorlton.

•DISTANCE•	6 miles (9.7km)
•MINIMUM TIME•	2hrs 30min
•ASCENT / GRADIENT•	1,098ft (335m) ▲▲▲
•LEVEL OF DIFFICULTY•	👫 👫 👫
•PATHS•	Tracks and moorland paths, lots of bracken, 11 stiles
•LANDSCAPE•	Farmland and moorland, with some woodland
•SUGGESTED MAP•	aqua3 OS Outdoor Leisure 26 North York Moors – Western
•START / FINISH•	Grid reference: NZ 477020
•DOG FRIENDLINESS•	Can be off lead on moorland and in woodland
•PARKING•	Roadside parking in Swainby village
•PUBLIC TOILETS•	None on route

BACKGROUND TO THE WALK

The charming and peaceful village street of Swainby, divided by its tree-lined stream, gives few hints of its dramatic past. It owes its existence to tragedy – the coming of plague – the Black Death – in the 14th century, when the inhabitants of the original village, just up the hill at Whorlton, deserted their homes and moved here. There may already have been a few houses here as Swainby means the village of the land workers, and is recorded in the 13th century. In the 19th century Swainby was shocked out of its peaceful, rural existence by the opening of the ironstone mines in Scugdale. The village took on many of the aspects of an American frontier town, becoming full of miners and their equipment, and awash with their smoke and clatter.

Jet Propelled

As well as ironstone, jet was mined in the Swainby area in the 19th century, including on Whorl Hill, which you will walk around. Most of the jet pits were small, employing no more than a dozen men, but they could be very profitable, especially during the boom time for jet, encouraged by the example of Queen Victoria's black mourning jewellery. Like coal, jet is fossilised wood. It comes in two types, hard and soft; hard jet was probably formed in sea water and soft jet in fresh water. It has been prized for more than 3,000 years, and was known to the Celts as Freya's Tears. Because it is easy to work and takes a fine polish, jet workshops could turn out large quantities of jewellery relatively quickly. Although some jet objects are still made, especially in Whitby, the industry had virtually died out by the 1920s.

Church and Castle

The path from Whorl Hill takes us into the deserted village of Whorlton. Little survived its abandonment after the Black Death except the church and the castle, both now partially ruined. On any but a sunny day, Holy Cross Church can be a disturbing place, with its avenue of yew trees leading to the arches of the nave, now open to the skies. The chancel is roofed, and a flap in the doorway allows you to look inside to see a fine early 14th-century oak figure of a knight. It is probably Nicholas, Lord Maynell, who fought with Edward I in Wales and hunted in the woods here. The gatehouse of the Maynell's castle, just along the road, is the only substantial part left. It was built at the end of the 14th century, and was besieged 250 years later during the Civil War. You can still see the marks of cannon balls from the Parliamentarians' guns on the walls. East of the castle, which occupied more than 6 acres (2.4 ha), are further earthworks, which protected the fortified village.

Walk 22 **Directions**

① With the church on your left, walk down the village street to the right of the stream. Continue past a sign 'Unsuitable for Coaches' and straight ahead uphill. As the road bends to the right, follow the bridleway sign to **Scugdale**, up the track ahead.

② Go through two gates, turning left after the second to join the waymarks for the the **Cleveland Way** National Trail. Walk through the woodland, turning left, just after a bench, down to a stile. The footpath goes downhill across the fields to another gate. Cross the stream on the footbridge to reach a lane, with another footbridge, over **Scugdale Beck**.

WHILE YOU'RE THERE ℹ
Spend a moment of solitude at nearby **Mount Grace Priory**, the best preserved of England's charterhouses – communities of Carthusian monks. There's a reconstructed monk's cell showing how they lived as hermits, coming together rarely except for services in the church. Their isolation was such that even their meals were served through an L-shaped hatch so they couldn't see who brought them.

③ Follow the lane past **Hollin Hill Farm** to a T-junction with telephone and post boxes. Cross the lane and go through a **Cleveland Way** signed gate. Walk up the path beside woodland to a gate with a stile beside it (there's a view of the valley from this ridge).

④ The path turns right to a stile and goes on to a paved track in the wood. Go straight ahead at a crossing track to another stile, and continue to follow the paved path on to the heather moorland. After the first summit, the path descends beyond a cairn into a dip. After the paved path ends, look out for a narrow path off to the left, down through the heather.

⑤ After about 100yds (91m) you will reach a concrete post where the path forks. Take the left fork and follow the path down the gully to a fence beside a wall. Turn left, forking left again down another gully to a signpost by a wall and fence. Follow the sign left and go over a spoil heap to reach a gate on your right.

⑥ Through the gate, go straight down the hill through woodland. At the bottom cross a stile by a gate and go down the lane. Just past a drive, where woodland begins, take a footpath over two stiles.

⑦ Walk up through the woodland on to a grassy track. Turn left, and left again at another track. At a T-junction, turn left again and follow the track downhill to a stile. Go straight ahead through a waymarked gateway.

WHERE TO EAT AND DRINK ℹ
The **Blacksmith's Arms** in Swainby, established in 1775, offers good beer and an extensive menu – though it no longer offers to shoe your horse. The **Black Horse** in the High Street is also noted for its beer.

⑧ Go over a stile beside a gate and follow the track along the hillside. Over a stile with steps beyond, turn left at the bottom and follow the field edge. Go over a waymarked stile by a gate and along the field. Walk along the field to a gate at the end, then follow the metalled lane past **Whorlton church** and castle back to **Swainby** village.

WHAT TO LOOK FOR ℹ
From the highest part of the walk, which takes you up on to the northern edge of the North York Moors plateau, you are rewarded with extensive northward views over the vast industrial complexes surrounding **Middlesbrough**. It was the production of iron from the hills which really put Middlesbrough on the map; it had a population of just 40 in 1829, 7,600 in 1851, when the first blast furnace opened, and 20,000 nine years later. Prime Minister Gladstone called the town 'an infant Hercules'. Beyond the River Tees, the area of **Seal Sands** is home to an oil refinery and chemical works. It's the terminal of the 220 mile (352km) pipeline bringing oil and gas from the Ekofisk field in the North Sea. If you are on the hills at dawn or dusk, you may see the flare stacks glowing on the skyline.

Out on the Tiles at Boltby and Thirlby Bank

Looking out for village mosaics and distant views on a quiet section of the Cleveland Way National Trail.

•DISTANCE•	5¼ miles (8.4km)
•MINIMUM TIME•	2hrs
•ASCENT / GRADIENT•	656ft (200m) ▲▲▲
•LEVEL OF DIFFICULTY•	🚶🚶🚶
•PATHS•	Mostly easy field and woodland paths; very steep and muddy climb up Thirlby Bank, 10 stiles
•LANDSCAPE•	Farmland, woodland and moorland ridge
•SUGGESTED MAP•	aqua3 OS Outdoor Leisure 26 North York – Western
•START / FINISH•	Grid reference: SE 490866
•DOG FRIENDLINESS•	Dogs should be on lead throughout but can probably be off on Cleveland Way
•PARKING•	Roadside parking in Boltby village
•PUBLIC TOILETS•	None on route

BACKGROUND TO THE WALK

The western boundary of the North York Moors National Park passes just outside the village of Boltby. It is a delightful, small-scale place, with a tiny 19th-century chapel and stone-built houses with red, pantiled roofs typical of the area. Despite its size, it used to have two pubs, as well as a tailor, a shoemaker, a butcher, a blacksmith and three masons. The single village street is crossed by the Gurtof Beck – pedestrians have their own ancient humpbacked stone bridge, from where the walk begins.

Mosaic Trail

As you begin the walk you will notice a glittering mosaic of a kingfisher on a wall beside the Gurtof Beck. This is one of 23 that mark points on the Hambleton Hillside Mosaic Walk. This 36 mile (57.5km) route begins at the National Park visitor centre at Sutton Bank, and winds its way on and off the ridge. Further on in the walk you'll come across a tiled picture of a red-capped mushroom on a tree stump, and a search of Boltby village on your return will yield a dragonfly and a worm-eating mole.

Moat and Park

The farm at Tang Hall has more ancient origins than you might think. Just before you reach it, you will notice deep ditches beside the path, sometimes filled with water. These are the remains of a moat which once surrounded a medieval manor house on the site. A little further on, the parkland of Southwoods Hall is typical of the managed landscapes of the 18th century. There are fine beech, lime and larch trees, as well as a cedar of Lebanon.

Beyond Southwoods Hall the walk passes through Midge Holme Gate and into woodland. This is very much pheasant country, and you are likely to flush out one or two of these noisy birds during the walk. Most characteristic is the male common pheasant, with its iridescent neck feathers of blue and green, its red wattles and long, arching tail. In contrast to the cock, the hen is duller – mottled brown and with a shorter tail. They are heavily protected from predators and poachers in these woods by gamekeepers, and kept well-fed during the winter months so that plenty survive for the shooting season, which begins on 1st October each year.

Fort and Lost
On top of Boltby Scar, just as you begin to descend from the Cleveland Way back to the village, are the scant remains of a Bronze Age hill fort, one of several along the edge of the Moors. It was 2.5 acres (1ha) in extent, and surrounded by an earth rampart and ditch on three of its five sides – the others were protected by the cliffs. It was mostly destroyed by ploughing in the late 1950s.

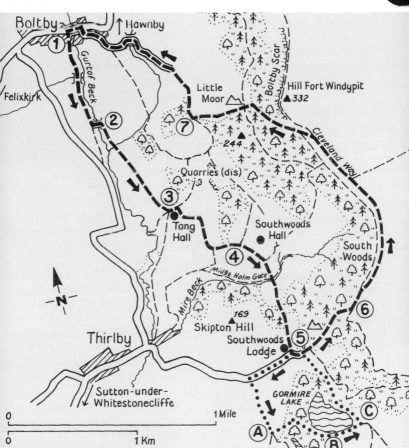

Walk 23 Directions

① From the humped-back bridge in the centre of **Boltby** village, follow the signed public footpath along the stream to a gate, and through three more gates to pass over a small footbridge to a stile. Continue following the stream, going over another three stiles, to cross a stone footbridge.

Walk 23

② Continue over two stiles, then turn right to another stile beside a gateway. Continue ahead, crossing a plank across a drainage ditch. Cross the field to a stile and a stone bridge. At another stile in a crossing fence, go straight ahead through the next field to reach a waymarked gate. Continue along the side of the field to a wooden stile, then through a gate on to a metalled track.

③ Turn left and, at the end of the farm buildings, turn right by a sign to **Southwoods** and through a gate to go diagonally across the field. Bend left at a waymarked wooden gate to continue with a wire fence on your right. The path veers left and descends to a gate.

> **WHILE YOU'RE THERE** ℹ
> Follow the scar south to visit the **White Horse** at Kilburn. From the car park at its foot you can ascend steps alongside the figure. Unlike most such figures, it is not cut from chalk, so it takes toil and ingenuity to keep it white and well-groomed. Some 314ft (95m) long and 228ft (69m) high, it was cut by the local schoolmaster, Thomas Hodgson and 30 helpers in 1857. He was said to have been impressed by a visit to the famous White Horse at Uffington in Oxfordshire.

④ Continue through another gateway and past a house. Continue along the metalled track, and across a crossing track to a gate. Confusingly this old track is named **Midge Holm Gate**. Follow the track to reach another gate beside a cottage, **Southwoods Lodge**, and go on to a metalled lane.

⑤ Turn left here, following the track, then turn left up a public footpath, signposted to **Thirlby Bank**. This is a steep and often

> **WHAT TO LOOK FOR** ℹ
> Look up during the walk and you are likely to see gliders soaring and circling overhead. They come from the **Yorkshire Gliding Club** at the top of Roulston Scar, beside Sutton Bank. The club was founded in 1934 and counts aviation ace Amy Johnson among its former members. In her day, the winch used to launch the gliders was a Rolls Royce Silver Ghost, bought and converted for just £100. If you want to experience the thrill of riding the thermals, the club operates all through the year – if weather allows – and offers 20-minute trial flights.

muddy track that ascends the ridge, past another public bridleway sign to reach a **Cleveland Way** sign at the top.

⑥ Turn left and follow the long distance footpath for about a mile (1.6km) along the ridge, until you reach a public bridleway sign to the left, to **Boltby**. Descend to a gate then follow the woodland ride, crossing a track to a gate. Continue ahead down the field, through a gate, and follow the track round to the right.

⑦ At a signpost, turn right towards **Boltby**, to continue to a gate. Pass a tree stump with a mosaic of a toadstool and descend to a gate on to a lane. Cross the stream by a footbridge and continue up the metalled lane. At the T-junction in the village, turn left back to the hump-backed bridge where the walk began.

> **WHERE TO EAT AND DRINK** ℹ
> There is nowhere on the route, but nearby is the **Sutton Bank visitor centre** which has a decent café. In Felixkirk, on the west side of Boltby, the **Carpenters Arms** at the top of the village serves good food in the bar or the restaurant.

Boltby and the Remote Gormire Lake

An extended version of Walk 23 visits Gormire Lake, an unusual survivor from the Ice Ages.
See map and information panel for Walk 23

·DISTANCE·	1¼ miles (2km)
·MINIMUM TIME·	3hrs 30min
·ASCENT / GRADIENT·	754ft (230m) ▲▲▲
·LEVEL OF DIFFICULTY·	🚶🚶🚶

Walk 24 Directions (Walk 23 option)

Gormire Lake is one of very few truly natural stretches of open water in North Yorkshire.

At Point ⑤ in Walk 23, at **Southwoods Lodge**, turn right on the metalled lane. After ¼ mile (400m) turn left at a bridleway sign before houses, and down a track. Go through a metal handgate beside a farm gate and up the grassy track to another handgate. Go across the field. Turn left at a waymark (Point Ⓐ), and continue with the hedge on the left. The path descends through woodland, over a wooden stile, bearing left after it.

Continue through woodland, now climbing, following a sign to **Gormire Lake**, eventually descending to the water's edge, Point Ⓑ.

Gormire was formed after the last Ice Age, when meltwater from the ice sheet that covered the Vale of York found its way blocked and collected in the depression formed.

Accessible only on foot, the lake is edged in summer with a wide variety of plants including the tufted loosestrife. Among the birds that you may see is the great crested grebe. In the dusk, beware if you hear the sound of horses; Gormire is said to be haunted by the ghost of a knight who tricked the Abbot of Rievaulx into lending him a horse, and plunged over Whitestone Cliff to his death in the lake, pursued by the devil.

At the water's edge you should turn right to reach a signpost, Point Ⓒ. Follow the footpath sign left to continue along the other side of the lake, then ascend to another signpost. Follow the **Southwoods** sign to rejoin the lakeside. After climbing and descending again, take a path to the right signed **Thirlby Bank** just before reaching Point ⑤ on the main walk again.

Walk 25

The Brontës at Thorpe Underwood

In the footsteps of Anne and Branwell Brontë, who spent time near Thorpe.

•DISTANCE•	4 miles (6.4km)
•MINIMUM TIME•	2hrs
•ASCENT / GRADIENT•	Negligible
•LEVEL OF DIFFICULTY•	
•PATHS•	Field paths and lanes, 8 stiles
•LANDSCAPE•	Flat farmland
•SUGGESTED MAP•	aqua3 OS Explorer 289 Leeds, Harrogate, Wetherby & Pontefract
•START / FINISH•	Grid reference: SE 459591
•DOG FRIENDLINESS•	Dogs should be on leads except on metalled tracks around Green Hammerton
•PARKING•	Wide verges beside lane, near Thorpe Underwood Water Meadows Fishing Centre
•PUBLIC TOILETS•	None on route

Walk 25 Directions

Walk along the lane with the **Thorpe Underwood Water Meadows Fishing Centre** to your left, to reach a **Green Hammerton** footpath sign on the right by a high brick wall. This is the edge of the Thorpe Underwood estate. Now home to an independent school, Thorpe Underwood Hall was rebuilt in 1912 on the site of the former Thorp Green Hall, where Anne Brontë was governess to the four children of the Revd Edmund

---

WHERE TO EAT AND DRINK ⓘ
There is nowhere directly on the route, though the **Bay Horse** in Green Hammerton is nearby. It serves real ale and has a beer garden. Food is served at lunchtime and in the evening. On the A59 York to Harrogate road there is a **Little Chef** restaurant at Skip Bridge, near Kirk Hammerton.

Robinson from 1840 to 1845. She had mixed feelings about her position. While she liked the children, she hated being away from her home in Haworth – her poem *Lines Written at Thorp Green* tells of her loneliness here.

Go over the stile beside the wall and follow the path between the hedge and wall, then straight ahead. Pass an equestrian water-jump and head half right to a stile in the top right-hand corner of the field, beside a wood. Look back to see something of the Thorp Green landscape. In 1843 Anne's brother Branwell was engaged as tutor to the Robinson's boy. Branwell was ill while he was there – but not so unwell that he was unable to instigate some sort of illicit relationship with Mrs Robinson. Her husband found out and Branwell was dismissed in July 1845; Anne had resigned a month earlier.

> **WHILE YOU'RE THERE** ℹ
> Visit the nearby village of **Aldborough**, by the River Ure north west of Thorpe Underwood. Set around a green with an ancient church, it is a prosperous and pretty place – and sent two members to Parliament before the Reform Act of 1832. Its origins are much older, though. It was a Roman town, Isurium Brigantium, developing from a camp set up by the Ninth Legion. It's still possible to trace much of the town's outline, and see two mosaic pavements. The little museum contains a collection of finds.

Go over the footbridge and follow the waymarked path diagonally across the field to pass between two oak trees. Continue with a hedge and fence to your right for 10yds (9m), then go over a waymarked stile on your right. Go diagonally right across the field to a footbridge in the hedge opposite. Go over the stile at the end of the bridge and follow the hedge on your right, over another two stiles and a footbridge.

Continue beside a small wood, over another stile, to a waymark post, then straight ahead across the field towards the farm buildings. The path curves to pass to the right of the buildings. After passing through a gateway by a footpath sign for **Thorpe Underwood**, turn left at a crossroads down a metalled road. Where the lane divides go, straight ahead through a gateway and continue along the metalled track. Just after the track passes over a stream, take a stile on the left to walk diagonally across the field, making for the right-hand side of the farm buildings. Go through an iron gate on to the farm track and follow the track as it turns right by a willow tree. Continue along the track, which swings left then continues straight ahead. This is part of the route by which Anne Brontë would have made her way from Thorp Green Hall to the railway at Cattal, on the York to Harrogate line, for her rare visits back to her home in Haworth.

Where the main track swings left, go straight on up a lesser track. The track passes beside woodland to a metal gate and comes out on to a lane. Go straight ahead to reach a high brick wall. Behind the wall, and just visible a little further on, is the 'new' Hall, designed in 1912 by York architect Walter Brierley, 'the Lutyens of the North'. The site of Thorp Green Hall was just to the north east of it, overlooking a large circular fishpond, of which Anne Brontë had a view from her room.

Follow the wall to a T-junction and turn left. Continue to follow the brick wall, turning left again at the next T-junction, just beyond the post box, and continue along the lane back to the parking place.

> **WHAT TO LOOK FOR** ℹ
> Anne Brontë, in *Agnes Grey*, said of the area 'The surrounding countryside itself was pleasant, as far as fertile fields, flourishing trees, quiet green lanes, and smiling hedges with wild flowers scattered along their banks, could make it; but it was depressingly flat to one born and nurtured among the rugged hills.' She enjoyed the local walks and her visits to the church at Little Ouseburn, a mile from the Hall. There is a drawing of the bridge that leads to the village by Anne, and also one of the church itself, where the Robinsons once had a private pew and where young Edmund, taught by both Anne and Branwell, was buried in 1869. He was 37 when he died – 20 years later than his tutors. Beside the church is the elegant circular mausoleum of another local family, the Thompsons of Kirby Hall.

Herriot's Darrowby

James Herriot based his fictional home town on his real one – Thirsk.

•DISTANCE•	5 miles (8km)
•MINIMUM TIME•	2hrs
•ASCENT / GRADIENT•	66ft (20m)
•LEVEL OF DIFFICULTY•	
•PATHS•	Town paths, field paths and tracks, 6 stiles
•LANDSCAPE•	Streamside and undulating pastureland around town
•SUGGESTED MAP•	aqua3 OS Explorer 302 Northallerton & Thirsk
•START / FINISH•	Grid reference: SE 430813
•DOG FRIENDLINESS•	Keep dogs on lead
•PARKING•	Roadside parking in the main street of Sowerby village
•PUBLIC TOILETS•	Thirsk town centre

BACKGROUND TO THE WALK

The elegant Georgian village street of Sowerby – now joined on to the town of Thirsk – is lined with a handsome avenue of lime trees. Such a civilised aspect belies the origins of the village's name, for Sowerby means the 'township in the muddy place'. Once you begin the walk, the reason becomes evident, even in dry weather. Sowerby is on the edge of the flood plain of the Cod Beck. Sowerby Flatts, which you will see across the beck at the start of the walk, and cross at the finish, is a popular venue for impromptu games of soccer and other sports, but is still prone to flooding.

Between Old and New

Once you've crossed the road by the end of New Bridge, you are walking between Old Thirsk and New Thirsk – though new in this context still means medieval. Old Thirsk is set to the east of the Cod Beck; like Sowerby, it too has a watery name, for Thirsk comes from an old Swedish word meaning a 'fen'. New Thirsk, to the west, is centred on the fine cobbled market place. The parish church, which you will pass twice, is the best Perpendicular church in North Yorkshire, with a particularly imposing tower.

South Kilvington, at the northern end of the walk, used to be a busy village on the main road north from Thirsk to Yarm. For much of the 19th century it was home to William Kingsley, who was vicar here until his death at the age of 101 in 1916 – having been born as Wellington defeated Napoleon at Waterloo. He entertained both the painter Turner and the art critic John Ruskin here – as well as his cousin Charles Kingsley, author of *The Water Babies*. More than a little eccentric, the Vicar had signs in his garden saying 'Beware of Mantraps'. When asked where they were, he paraded his three housemaids.

Darrowby and Wight

For many visitors, the essential place to visit in Thirsk is Skeldale House in Kirkgate – on the right as you return from the church to the Market Square. This was the surgery of local vet James Wight – better known by his pen name, James Herriot. Now an award-winning museum, 'The World of James Herriot', this was where Wight worked for all his professional life. Thirsk itself is a major character in the books, appearing lightly disguised as Darrowby.

The museum has reconstructions of what the surgery and the family rooms were like in the 1940s, and tells the history of veterinary science. Whether or not you're a fan of the Herriot tales, which began with *If Only They Could Talk* in 1970, you'll find it a fascinating and nostalgic tour.

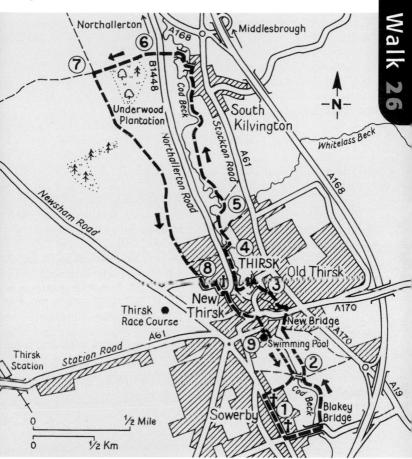

Walk 26 **Directions**

① Walk down the village street, away from **Thirsk**. Just past the Methodist Church on the left, go left down **Blakey Lane**. After the bridge turn left through a kissing gate and go through four kissing gates to reach a footbridge.

② Continue along the path, with the stream on your left, to a stile and go through two gates to a car park, keeping straight ahead to the road. Cross it and take a path that curves left then right by the bridge. At a paved area turn right, to go alongside a green to a road.

③ Cross and continue beside the houses, going left at the top of the green. Cross the metal bridge and continue beside the beck opposite the east end of the church. Before reaching the road take the path to the right, beside a bench, to a footbridge on the right.

Walk 26

④ Cross the bridge, go through two gates and curve left to follow the beck to a gate by a bridge. Go straight ahead (not over the bridge) and follow the path across the fields, veering slightly right to a stile on your right.

⑤ Go over the stile and follow the stream, going over another two stiles to pass beside houses. Continue left over a footbridge by some mill buildings. The path winds right to a second footbridge. Follow the bridleway sign across the field through two more gates to reach the main road.

⑥ Cross the road and go through a signed gate opposite, to another gate beside a wood. At an open space past the wood, turn left through a gap in the hedge, opposite a waymark to the right.

⑦ Walk down the field with a hedge on your left. In the second field go left over a stile and continue with the hedge on your right to another stile. Bear left to meet a path that crosses the field and becomes a grassy lane between hedges, then a track.

⑧ At a metalled road go straight ahead, bearing left then right past the church tower. Turn right and walk into the town centre. In the

Market Place head half left towards the Three Tuns Inn, and down a signed passageway by the drycleaners.

⑨ Cross the road diagonally right and go towards the swimming pool entrance. Turn left and bend round the pool building to a gate. Go ahead to a gate and alongside the beck. At the bridge turn right across the field on a grassy track to a gate on to a lane. Go straight ahead to return to **Sowerby** village street.

WHERE TO EAT AND DRINK ⓘ

Thirsk has a good choice of cafés, pubs and hotels. Recommended are the up-market **Golden Fleece** and the **Three Tuns** in the Market Place. The **Lord Nelson** has bar meals and Sunday lunches, while **Yorks Tea Rooms**, also in the Market Place, offers good lunches and a range of coffees. In Sowerby, **Sheppard's Hotel and Restaurant** offers lunch and dinner.

WHILE YOU'RE THERE ⓘ

Visit the **Thirsk Museum and tourist information centre** at 14 Kirkgate. As well as having interesting local exhibits and displays, this was the birthplace, in November 1756, of Thomas Lord. The son of a local farmer, Thomas made his name as a professional cricketer, and set up his own ground in Dorset Square in 1787. Lord's Cricket Ground moved to its present site in 1814.

WHAT TO LOOK FOR ⓘ

See if you can catch a film at the **Ritz Cinema**, just off the Market Place. Built in 1912, it went under several names during its 80-year history, finally closing in 1992 as Studio One. For the previous ten years it had been kept going by a dedicated husband and wife team, but the economics of local cinemas had become almost impossible. The people of Thirsk were determined to have films back in their town, however, and, under the control of Thirsk Town Council, it was reopened in March 1995, reverting to its original name and on a six-month lease. So successful was it, that it still continues to show a regular programme of films. It is now run entirely by volunteers. Its equipment – including a horn-shaped loudspeaker above the screen dating from the 1930s – has been updated, but the Ritz still retains the atmosphere of a typical small-town cinema of the past.

A Medieval Walk from Fountains

From the magnificent ruins of Fountains Abbey to the fascinating medieval manor of Markenfield Hall.

•DISTANCE•	6½ miles (10.4km)
•MINIMUM TIME•	3hrs
•ASCENT / GRADIENT•	328ft (100m) ▲▲ ▲
•LEVEL OF DIFFICULTY•	🚶 🚶 🚶
•PATHS•	Field paths and tracks, a little road walking, 8 stiles
•LANDSCAPE•	Farmland and woodland
•SUGGESTED MAP•	aqua3 OS Explorer 298 Nidderdale
•START / FINISH•	Grid reference: SE 270681
•DOG FRIENDLINESS•	Dogs should be on leads on field paths, can be off lead in parts of woodland
•PARKING•	Car park at west end of Abbey, or at visitor centre
•PUBLIC TOILETS•	Fountains Abbey visitor centre

BACKGROUND TO THE WALK

After you have climbed the hill from the car park and begun the walk along the valley side, following the ancient abbey wall, the south front of Fountains Hall is below you. Built by Sir Stephen Proctor in 1611, it is a fine Jacobean House, with lots of mullioned windows and cross gables. Were it anywhere other than at the entrance to Fountains Abbey it would be seen as one of the great houses of the age. Sir Stephen was, by all accounts, not the most scrupulous of men, having made his huge fortune as Collector of Fines on Penal Statutes. Nor did he respect the Abbey buildings; the stone he built his house with was taken from the south east corner of the monastic remains.

Abbey and Abbot

A little further along the path, the Abbey ruins come into view. When monks from St Mary's Abbey in York first settled here in 1132 it was a wild and desolate place. Nevertheless their abbey prospered, and became one of the country's richest and most powerful Cistercian monasteries. More remains of Fountains than of any other abbey ruin in the country. Its church was 360ft (97.5m) long. The other buildings, laid out along (and over) the River Skell, give a vivid impression of what life was like here in the Middle Ages. All came to an end in 1539 when King Henry VIII dissolved the larger monasteries. This was only a few years after Abbot Marmaduke Huby had built the huge tower, a symbol of what he believed was the enduring power of his abbey.

Mr Aislabie's Garden

Beyond Fountains Abbey are the pleasure gardens laid out between 1716 and 1781 by John Aislabie and his son William. John had retired to his estate here at Studley Royal after being involved – as Chancellor of the Exchequer – in the financial scandal of the South Sea Bubble. It is one of the great gardens of Europe, contrasting green lawn with stretches of water, both formal and informal. Carefully placed in the landscape are ornamental buildings, from classical temples to Gothic towers. The Aislabie's mansion stood at the north end of the park; it was destroyed by fire in 1945.

The highlight of the southern end of the walk is Markenfield Hall, a rare early 14th-century fortified manor house, built around 1310 for the Markenfield family. You can see the tomb of Sir Thomas Markenfield and his wife Dionisia in Ripon Cathedral. Open on Mondays during the summer, the house still clearly demonstrates how a medieval knight and his family lived; it is part home, part farm. You can still see the chapel and the hall. The gatehouse, convincingly medieval, is actually early 20th century.

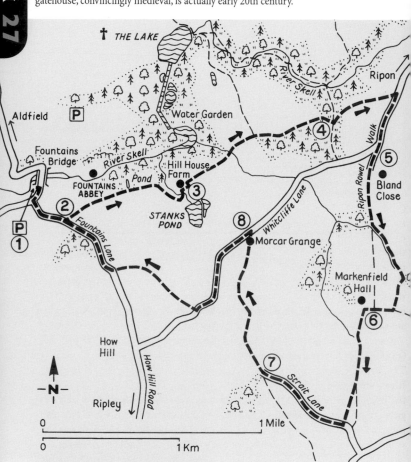

Walk 27 **Directions**

① From the car park turn right uphill, signed '**Harrogate**'. At the fork go left, signed '**Markington, Harrogate**'. Just after the road bends right, go over a stile beside a gate with bridleway signs.

② Follow the grassy path just inside the ancient **Abbey Wall**, past a small pond. Go through a waymarked gate and follow the track as it curves round to the right through another gate then left round the farm buildings of **Hill House Farm**. Go through a small gate near the farm house.

WHAT TO LOOK FOR ℹ

Clearly visible from much of the walk is the spire of **St Mary's Church** in Studley Park. Now in the care of English Heritage, it was designed for the 1st Marquess of Ripon by the Victorian architect William Burges, between 1871 and 1878, at a cost of £15,000. It was money well spent. Where the exterior is restrained, the interior glows with colour and imagery. A dome over the altar is painted with angels. A carved, winged lion peers from the arches in the chancel. Mosaics show the heavenly city in the flooring. A brass door has a statue of the Virgin and Child. Burges's decoration gets richer from west to east, but throughout the church there is glowing, colourful stained glass. Even the organ seems to be trying to make a statement. In a corner of the south aisle is the alabaster tomb of the Marquess and his wife.

③ Turn right then follow the footpath signs to go left at the end of a large shed and then right. Go through a metalled gate on to a track. At the end of the hedge go ahead down the field to a gate into the wood. Follow the track, passing the ruined archway, to descend to a crossroads.

④ Go straight on, signed 'Ripon'. The track climbs to a gate with a **Ripon Rowel Walk** sign. Follow the track beside the line of trees to a gate on to **Whitcliffe Lane**. Turn right. At the top of the rise go straight ahead on the metalled road.

⑤ Go over the cattle grid by **Bland Close**, then straight ahead with the hedge on your right to reach a stile. Continue along the waymarked track, eventually with woodland to your right. Go over a stile near a metal gate and follow the track as it goes right to reach a gate. Turn right to some farm buildings by **Markenfield Hall**.

WHILE YOU'RE THERE ℹ

As well as visiting the Abbey and the gardens, take the time to visit nearby **Ripon**. Its cathedral has a Saxon crypt, and in the stately market place is Britain's oldest free-standing obelisk, designed in 1702 by Hawksmoor. You can discover Ripon's links with Lewis Carroll and how it inspired his Alice books, and see how the law was administered and the wicked punished on the Law and Order Trail.

⑥ Follow the wall to the left, going through a metal gate and straight ahead down the track, through a gate. Follow the track, then a waymark sign, across a field to a stile by a gate. Turn right up the narrow **Strait Lane**, to emerge into a field.

⑦ Follow the waymarked path beside a field. Go through a gate in the field corner and continue ahead with the hedge to the right. Go through four more gates and follow the track as it curves towards farm buildings. Go over a stile into the farmyard of **Morcar Grange**, and ahead to the metalled **Whitecliffe Lane**.

⑧ Turn left and follow the lane as it bends left then right. At the next corner, look for a stile on the right beside a gate. Cross the field half left and go over three stiles, following the waymarked path towards the buildings. Go over a stile and pass between the buildings to reach a metalled road. Turn back to the car park.

WHERE TO EAT AND DRINK ℹ

The **National Trust's visitor centre** has a pleasant, airy restaurant offering snacks and meals. There is also a café at the east end of the gardens, near the lake. Nearby Ripon offers a wider choice of pubs, restaurants and tea rooms.

Walk 28

Richmond's Drummer Boy

Following in the steps of the Richmond Drummer, to Easby Abbey.

•**DISTANCE**•	6 miles (9.7km)
•**MINIMUM TIME**•	2hrs 20min
•**ASCENT / GRADIENT**•	656ft (200m) ▲▲▲
•**LEVEL OF DIFFICULTY**•	🚶 🚶 🚶
•**PATHS**•	Field and riverside paths, a little town walking, 20 stiles
•**LANDSCAPE**•	Valley of River Swale and its steep banks
•**SUGGESTED MAP**•	aqua3 OS Explorer 304 Darlington & Richmond
•**START / FINISH**•	Grid reference: NZ 168012
•**DOG FRIENDLINESS**•	Dogs should be on leads for most of walk
•**PARKING**•	Friars Close long-stay car park
•**PUBLIC TOILETS**•	Friars Close car park and Round Howe car park

BACKGROUND TO THE WALK

The first part of the walk follows much of the route taken by the legendary Richmond Drummer Boy. At the end of the 18th century, the story says, soldiers in Richmond Castle discovered a tunnel that was thought to lead from there to Easby Abbey. They sent their drummer boy down it, beating his drum so they could follow from above ground. His route went under the Market Square and along to Frenchgate, then beside the river towards the abbey. At the spot now marked by the Drummer Boy Stone, the drumming stopped. The Drummer Boy was never seen again. Now the walk is re-enacted each year, with a local schoolboy playing the drum (but walking above ground!). The Green Howards Regimental Museum in the Market Square can tell you more about the drummer boy and his regiment.

Abbey and church

Easby Abbey, whose remains are seen on your walk, was founded for Premonstratensian Canons in 1155 by the Constable of Richmond Castle. Although not much of the church remains, some of the other buildings survive well, including the gatehouse, built about 1300. The refectory is also impressive, and you can see the infirmary, the chapter house and the dormitory. Just by the abbey ruins is the parish church, St Agatha's. It contains a replica of the Anglo-Saxon Easby Cross (the original is in the British Museum) and a set of medieval wall paintings showing Old Testament scenes of Adam and Eve, on the north wall, and the life of Jesus on the south, as well as depictions of activities such as pruning and hawking.

After the Abbey, you'll cross the River Swale on the old railway bridge, and follow the track bed for a while. This was part of the branch line from Richmond to Darlington, which opened in 1846. It was closed in 1970. The station, a little further along the Catterick Road, is now a garden centre, and the engine shed a gym. Look right over Richmond Bridge as you cross, to see how the stonework differs from one end to the other. It was built by two different contractors, one working for Richmond Council and one for the North Riding of Yorkshire. In the hillside below Billy Bank Wood, which you enter beyond the bridge, were copper mines dating back to the 15th century. After you have climbed the hill and crossed the 12 stiles (between Points ⑤ and ⑥), you're following the old route of the Swale, which thousands of years ago changed its course and formed the hill known as Round Howe.

Walk **28**

Walk 28 Directions

① Leave the car park and turn right, then left at the T-junction. At the roundabout go left, then go right at the next roundabout down

Dundas Street, bending right into **Frenchgate** then left into **Station Road**. Just past the church, take **Lombards Wynd** left.

② Turn right at the next junction and follow the track, passing to the

Walk 28

right of the **Drummer Boy Stone** along the path. Leaving Richmond behind, go over two stiles and follow the waymarks towards the **Abbey** to another two stiles. Turn right along the track and right again, this time down the metalled lane which leads to the **Abbey** in the village of **Easby**.

③ Go to the left of the car park along the track. Where it divides, keep on the higher path, then go right by **Platelayers Cottage** over the old railway bridge. Follow the track bed for 400yds (366m), and go left over a cattle grid, to follow the track right, to the road.

> **WHERE TO EAT AND DRINK** ⓘ
> Richmond has many places for food and drink. The **King's Head Hotel** in the Market Square has meals, sandwiches and afternoon teas. One of the places that locals recommend is the **Frenchgate Café**, with its bistro-like atmosphere.

④ Turn right, and follow the road for ½ mile (800m). Turn left up **Priory Villas**, bearing right to go in front of the houses and through three gates. Keeping parallel to the river, cross some playing fields and pass a clubhouse to a road.

⑤ Cross the road, and take a signed path opposite, to the left of the cottage. Climb steeply through the

> **WHILE YOU'RE THERE** ⓘ
> Visit **Richmond Castle**, which looms over the Swale Valley through much of the walk. Its keep, more than 100ft (30m) high, was complete by 1180. Now in the care of English Heritage, the castle's central ward is surrounded by high curtain walls with towers. Inside the keep are unique drawings done in the First World War by conscientious objectors. They were imprisoned here in squalid conditions.

woodland, through a gate and a stile, bending right at the end of the woodland to a stile in a crossing fence. Turn right over the stile, and follow the signed path over 12 more stiles. Just before reaching a gate, go right through a wall gap and left to another stile.

⑥ Turn right, to go through a gate. Follow the track as it bends downhill to a bridge. Cross it and walk to the lane. Go left and left again at the main road. After 200yds (183m) go right up a gravel track, to a junction.

⑦ Turn right, and follow the track uphill, bearing right then left near the farmhouse, to reach a metalled lane. Turn right and follow the lane back into **Richmond**. Go ahead at the main road and follow it as it bends left to the garage, where you turn left back to the car park.

> **WHAT TO LOOK FOR** ⓘ
> **Wynds** are a feature of the Richmond townscape. A northern term, from the Old English word for 'to spiral', these narrow lanes usually link two wider streets. You'll see Friar's Wynd to your right, beside the Georgian Theatre Royal, as you begin the walk, and just after the parish church you will turn left along Lombard's Wynd. This was once part of the ancient route up from the banks of the River Swale to the north eastern area of the town around Frenchgate – 'Frankesgate' in the Middles Ages. Both these names suggest that this part of the town was once occupied by foreign workers; they may have been helping to build the castle. Finkle Street, that runs north west from the Market Place, has a name that is often found in Yorkshire towns and means 'crooked'. West of the Market Square is Newbiggin, the 'new settlement' – new, that is in 1071 when the castle was begun.

Richmond and the River Swale

To explore the valley of the River Swale a little further, take this extra loop to Whitcliffe Scar, with a taste of classic Swaledale landscape.
See map and information panel for Walk 28

•DISTANCE•	9¼ miles (14.9km)
•MINIMUM TIME•	3hrs 30min
•ASCENT / GRADIENT•	754ft (230m) ▲▲▲
•LEVEL OF DIFFICULTY•	🚶 🚶 🚶

Walk 29 Directions (Walk 28 option)

Richmond is the gateway to the wonderful northern dale of Swaledale. To catch a glimpse of this bewitchingly beautiful landscape you can follow the River Swale a bit further upstream then climb up to the impressive limestone crags of Whitcliffe Scar.

At Point ⑦ on the main walk, don't turn right but continue ahead along the track. Just before a farm, follow waymarks to go right to a stile, then follow the hedge to the left to another stile and on to the woodland track. Go right at the waymark, away from the river, to emerge from the woodland. Cross a wire fence on the left and half right to meet a grassy track, Point Ⓐ.

Turn right and follow the track parallel with the river and over two stiles to ascend to a third stile. Pass a barn, go over another stile and half right. You are now at the foot of **Deep Dale**, a dry valley cut by melting water from Ice Age glaciers on the heights rushing down to the

valley below. The moorland above you is part of the extensive army training area associated with Catterick Garrison a few miles away.

Go through a gap in the wall, and turn right to a stile by a gate, Point Ⓑ. Follow the sign straight ahead, then bend right by the ruined wall.

Cross the wall to a stile, cross the lane and go over another two stiles to turn right on a farm track. Above you is **Whitcliffe Scar**, from where Robert Willance fell in 1606 when his young horse bolted in the fog. The horse died but he survived, with a broken leg. Knowing that rescue would be some time coming, he slit open the horses belly and put his leg inside, keeping it warm and preventing gangrene. He lived, and the place became known as **Willance's Leap**.

A few paces down the track, go left over a stile and follow the track to a stile by a gate into woodland, Point Ⓒ. Leave the woodland by a gate, and go through two more gates. The lane becomes metalled and rejoins Walk 28 back into **Richmond** just beyond Point ⑦.

Walk 30

Romantic Hackfall – A Lost Landscape

Walking through a remarkable 18th-century Romantic landscape enjoyed in the 19th and neglected for much of the 20th.

•DISTANCE•	5½ miles (9km)
•MINIMUM TIME•	2hrs 15min
•ASCENT / GRADIENT•	623ft (190m) ▲ ▲ ▲
•LEVEL OF DIFFICULTY•	👫 👫 👫
•PATHS•	Woodland paths (muddy at all times), field tracks, 3 stiles
•LANDSCAPE•	Artificial Romantic garden, woods and river gorge
•SUGGESTED MAP•	aqua3 OS Explorer 298 Nidderdale
•START / FINISH•	Grid reference: SE 230765
•DOG FRIENDLINESS•	Dogs can be off lead in woodland
•PARKING•	Roadside parking in Grewelthorpe
•PUBLIC TOILETS•	None on route

Walk 30 Directions

From the village, walk up the road towards **Masham**. Just beyond the speed restriction sign, turn right over a plank bridge by the Woodland Trust sign. The path winds through the wood, and down stone steps. Ignore a stile on the left and continue down into the woods, alongside a gully. You are now in **Hackfall Woods**. Once among the most famous of gardens in England, it was painted by Turner, recommended by Wordsworth as a place to visit on the way to the Lake District – and was even depicted on a Wedgwood dinner service owned by Russian Empress Catherine the

Great. Laid out in the 1730s by William Aislabie as an antidote to the formality of his father's nearby Studley Royal, it attracted visitors right up to the 1920s.

During your walk you will see some of the buildings Aislabie built there, mostly Gothic follies and garden houses, now in disrepair. Hackfall was sold in 1932 to a timber merchant, who felled the beech trees and left the rest to moulder. Its rescue has come about through the Woodland Trust, which now manages it with a light hand and with the support of the local Hackfall Trust. Eventually the path takes a sharp right fork into the valley bottom to meet a main path, signed '**Ripon Rowel Walk**'.

Follow the path left across the stream, then take a right fork across a footbridge to see the **River Ure** on the right. This is one of the most spectacular stretches of the river, where it passes through a narrow

---

WHERE TO EAT AND DRINK ⓘ

The **Crown Inn** in Grewelthorpe, nearly 400 years old, serves home-cooked bar meals and also has a popular restaurant. It prides itself on its real ales. For a wider choice, the city of Ripon is only 20 minutes drive away.

Walk 30

gorge – a mid 19th-century guidebook spoke of 'the abyss at your feet, where the black waters sleep in cavernous gloom.'

Go through a gate, across a tiny footbridge, turn right through a gate in a wall and go back into the woods. The path rises and comes out of the woods at a signed gate. Go along the grassy track up to another gate and turn right along the track to reach farm buildings. Turn left, taking a track towards the road. At the top of the track turn left along a grassy track parallel with the road, and eventually join it. As the road bends left and the wood starts, go through a gate on the right with a Forestry Commission notice on it. Just after the gate, take a grassy track on the left, up through the wood to reach a stony track. Go left for a few paces, then continue uphill on the grassy track, to cross another stony track and bend slightly right to continue up the grassy path. At the edge of the woodland you will meet a track going left. Follow this track left for about 100yds (91m), then turn right down towards a small gate at the edge of the field.

Follow the path half left towards the top of the hill to a stile. Continue along the field side, with a hedge on the left, to another stile in the hedge. Go diagonally right across the field with a trig point to the left and over two more stiles. Near the trig point you may be able to make out the angle of the earthworks marking an early farming enclosure; its age has not been accurately determined. There are also wide views – Roseberry Topping is visible in clear weather. Go diagonally to the opposite corner of the field, veering away from the buildings to reach a road through two stone posts. Turn left along the road back to **Grewelthorpe**, where you might reflect on the 19th-century guidebook's words 'To those who are gladdened by the works of Nature, and a ramble in an umbrageous retreat, there cannot be afforded a richer treat than a trip to Hackfall.'

Walk 31

A Kingdom for a Horse

From Middleham Castle, favourite home of King Richard III, and back via the gallops for today's thoroughbreds.

•DISTANCE•	7 miles (11.3km)
•MINIMUM TIME•	2hrs 30min
•ASCENT / GRADIENT•	475ft (145m) ▲ ▲ ▲
•LEVEL OF DIFFICULTY•	🚶 🚶 🚶
•PATHS•	Field paths and tracks, with some road walking, 18 stiles
•LANDSCAPE•	Gentle farmland, riverside paths, views of Wensleydale
•SUGGESTED MAP•	aqua3 OS Outdoor Leisure 30 Yorkshire Dales – Northern & Central
•START / FINISH•	Grid reference: SE 127877
•DOG FRIENDLINESS•	Livestock and horses in fields, so dogs on leads
•PARKING•	In square in centre of Middleham
•PUBLIC TOILETS•	Middleham

BACKGROUND TO THE WALK

When Richard III died at the Battle of Bosworth Field in 1485, Middleham lost one of its favourite residents. Richard had lived here, in the household of the Earl of Warwick – The Kingmaker – when a boy, and set up home here with the Earl's daughter Anne after their marriage. As Duke of Gloucester, it was his power base as effective ruler of the North under his brother Edward IV. Locals don't believe the propagandist version of Richard, promoted by Shakespeare's play, that he was a murderer – the Lord Mayor of York reported to his council after Bosworth that 'King Richard, late lawfully reigning over us, was through great treason piteously slain and murdered.' Middleham Castle today is a splendid ruin, with one of the biggest keeps in England, impressive curtain walls and a deep moat. It is in the care of English Heritage.

From Middleham, the walk takes us to the River Cover and along its banks. After crossing Hullo Bridge the path ascends to Braithwaite Hall. Owned by the National Trust and open by appointment only, this is a modest farmhouse of 1667, with three fine gables and unusual oval windows beneath them. Inside are stone-flagged floors, a fine oak staircase and wood panelling all of the late 17th century. On the hillside behind are the earthworks of a hill fort, thought to be Iron Age. After the Hall, the lane eventually crosses Coverham Bridge, probably built by the monks of nearby Coverham Abbey. There are a few remains of the Abbey, founded in the 12th century, mostly incorporated into later buildings on the site. Miles Coverdale, who was the first man to complete a full English translation of the Bible, came from here.

Middleham – the Lambourn of the North

For many people, Middleham is the home of famous racehorses, and you may be lucky enough to see some in training as you walk over Middleham Low Moor towards the end of the walk – make sure you keep out of their way. More than 500 horses train in Middleham, under the watchful eyes of 13 trainers. Both the Low Moor and the High Moor have been used for exercise for more than 300 years; one of the earliest recorded winners was Bay

Bolton, born in 1705, which won Queen Anne's Gold Cup at York Races. Among early jockeys was the splendidly-named 'Crying Jackie' Mangle, who won the St Leger five times in the 1770s and 80s.

To your left as you leave the Low Moor and make your way back to the castle is William's Hill, the remains of the original motte and bailey castle built here by the Normans after 1066 to guard the approaches to Wensleydale and Coverdale. The motte, 40ft (12m) high, is joined by a curved bailey surrounded by a ditch. It was abandoned about 1170 when the new castle was begun nearby.

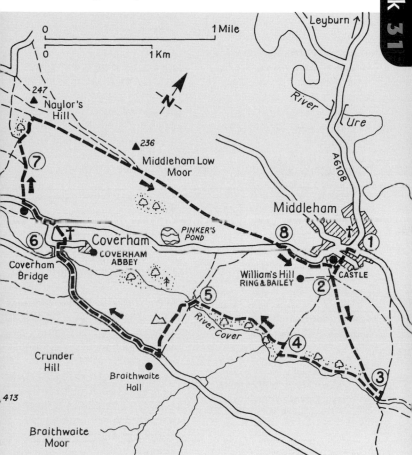

Walk 31 Directions

① From the cross in the **Square**, walk uphill past the **Black Swan Hotel**. A few paces beyond, turn left up a narrow passage beside the **Castle Tea Rooms**, continuing across the road and left of the **Castle** to a gate.

② Go half left across the field, following the sign pointing towards the stepping stones. Cross the next three fields, over the waymarked stiles. After the third field, turn along the side of the field, ignoring a track to the right. Turn right at a waymarked crossing wall down to the bank of the **River Cover** by the stepping stones.

Walk 31

③ Turn right (do not cross the stepping stones) and follow the riverside path, going through a gate and up some steps. After returning to the riverbank, go right where the path forks. Go over two more stiles, turning immediately right after the second. Follow the waymark uphill to a marker post.

④ Turn left and follow the line of the wood. At the end of the field go left through a waymarked stile, through the trees to a second stile, then straight down the field back to the river bank. Go over a waymarked stile and onward to the bridge.

WHAT TO LOOK FOR ℹ

If you are very lucky you may see the iridescent blue and orange of the **kingfisher**, fishing above the waters of the River Cover. Vulnerable both to pollution and the ravages of a harsh winter, the kingfisher lives in the banks of the river, digging out a burrow up to 3ft (1m) deep. At the end a nest is constructed for the female to lay six or seven eggs. Young kingfishers are fed mainly with small fish – minnow and sticklebacks. Kingfishers catch fish with their fearsome bills and carry them back to their perches overlooking the stream. They carefully turn them so the head faces outwards from the bill, and hit them against the perch to stun or kill them, before swallowing them whole.

⑤ Go through the gate over the bridge. Follow the track as it winds right and uphill through two gates on to a road, opposite **Braithwaite Hall**. Turn right, and follow the road for a mile (1.6km) to **Coverham Bridge**. Turn right over the bridge, then right again.

⑥ Before the gates, turn left through a small gate, walk beside a waterfall and into the churchyard.

WHILE YOU'RE THERE ℹ

Nearby **Wensley**, after which the dale takes its name, was once a market town, but plague in 1563 reduced it to this little village. Visit the church to see the monumental brass to the priest Simon de Wensley – one of the best in the country – and the wonderful out-of-place Scrope family pew, partly made of the rood screen from Easby Abbey near Richmond.

Leave by the lychgate and turn left along the road. After ¼ mile (400m) go through a gate on the right opposite a disused factory, bearing slightly left. Go over three stiles. Go through a gate, pass between buildings and go over three stiles through a belt of woodland.

⑦ Cross the field to a gateway right of the wood. After passing the house, bend left to a gate on to a track. Turn right, go through a gate and turn right again. Don't follow the track, but go half left to meet a bridleway across the moor. Follow it for 1½ miles (2.4km) to the road.

⑧ Turn left. Just before the **Middleham** sign, take a signposted path on the right. Turn left over the stile and follow the path parallel to the road. Go through two more stiles, then take another towards the castle, passing through a gate on to the lane. Turn left and return to the square.

WHERE TO EAT AND DRINK ℹ

Several of Middleham's hotels and inns offer meals and snacks as well as drinks. The **White Swan** has bar meals and a noted restaurant, open lunchtime and evenings. **Millers House Hotel** has dinners (weekends only in winter). The **Stable Door Restaurant** is open most lunchtimes and evenings and offers good home-cooked food.

The Mines of Greenhow and Bewerley Moor

Through a landscape of lead mining, from one of Yorkshire's highest villages.

·DISTANCE·	5¾ miles (9.2km)
·MINIMUM TIME·	2hrs 30min
·ASCENT / GRADIENT·	1,181ft (360m) ▲▲ ▲▲ ▲
·LEVEL OF DIFFICULTY·	秾 秾 秾
·PATHS·	Field and moorland paths and tracks, 3 stiles
·LANDSCAPE·	Moorland and valley, scarred by fascinating remains of the lead mining industry
·SUGGESTED MAP·	aqua3 OS Explorer 298 Nidderdale
·START / FINISH·	Grid reference: SE 114642
·DOG FRIENDLINESS·	Dogs can be off lead for much of the route
·PARKING·	Car park by Miners Arms
·PUBLIC TOILETS·	None on route

BACKGROUND TO THE WALK

It is a long haul from Pateley Bridge up Greenhow Hill to the village of Greenhow, one of the highest in Yorkshire, at around 1,300ft (396m) above sea level. Until the early 17th century this was all bleak and barren moorland. When lead mining on a significant scale developed in the area in the 1600s, a settlement was established here, though most of the surviving buildings are late 18th and 19th century. Many of the cottages also have a small piece of attached farmland, for the miners were also farmers, neither occupation alone giving them a stable income or livelihood. In a way typical of such mining villages, the church and the pub – the Miners Arms, of course – are at the very centre.

Romans and Monks

Romans are the first known miners of Greenhow, though there is said to be some evidence of even earlier activity, as far back as the Bronze Age. The Romans had a camp near Pateley Bridge, and ingots of lead – called 'pigs' – have been found nearby, dating from the 1st century AD. In the Middle Ages lead from Yorkshire became important for roofing castles and cathedrals – it is said that it was even used in Jerusalem. Production was governed by the major landowners, the monasteries, and some, like Fountains and Byland, became rich from selling charters for mining and from royalties. After the monasteries were dissolved, the new landowners wanted to exploit their mineral rights, and encouraged many small-scale enterprises in return for a share of the profits.

As you leave Greenhow and begin to descend into the valley of the Gill Beck, you pass through the remains of the Cockhill Mine. It is still possible to make out the dressing floor, where the lead ore was separated from the waste rock and other minerals, and the location of the smelt works, where the ore was processed. Beyond, by the Ashfold Side Beck, were the Merryfield Mines and, where the route crosses the beck, there are extensive remains of the Prosperous Smelt Mill. All these mines were active in the middle of the 19th century, and some had a brief resurgence in the mid 20th.

Walk 32

Besides the Lead

Coldstones Quarry, opposite you when you've reached the main road past Coldstones Farm, opened about 1900. It produces limestone – almost 1 million tonnes a year. Around Greenhow the limestone layers are particularly deep, allowing large blocks to be cut. Across it run two mineral veins, called Garnet Vein and Sun Vein, both of which have been mined in the past for lead and (later) for fluorite. Other minerals found in smaller quantities in the rock here are barite, calcite and galena, as well as crystals of cerrusite, anglesite and occasionally quartz.

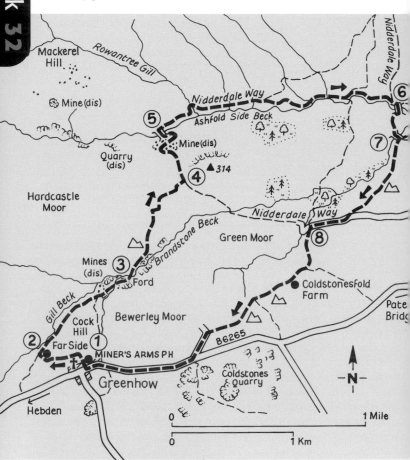

Walk 32 Directions

① Turn right out of the car park. After about 100yds (91m), just after a converted chapel, take a lane to the right. At the junction go left and follow the lane to a cattle grid and through a gate. Curve right, round behind the farmhouse.

② Follow the track downhill into the valley of **Gill Beck** and then **Brandstone Beck**, where there are the extensive remains of lead mining activity. Where the track swings left, go ahead down the valley to reach the main track near a concrete building. Go right of the building and just beyond go ahead down the valley to the ford.

WHILE YOU'RE THERE ℹ

Nearby **Stump Cross Caverns** can take you into the underground world below Greenhow. The limestone cave system was discovered in the middle of the 19th century. You can visit a succession of caves with plenty of stalagmites and stalactites, many with fanciful names, where ancient animal bones, including those of the wolverine, have been discovered. It is open daily from mid-March to mid-November.

③ Cross and follow the obvious track up the hill. Go over a stile beside a gate by trees then, 100yds (91m) beyond, take another stile on the right. Follow the track towards the farm, going left between stone walls, and descend to another stile on to a track.

④ Turn left and go through a waymarked gateway. By a spoil heap follow the track to the right and downhill. Veer slightly left, past an iron cogwheel, to cross **Ashfold Side Beck** on a concrete causeway to a gate.

⑤ Follow the bridleway sign to the right and climb the hill, to a **Nidderdale Way** sign, where you turn right along the track to a gate. Wind round the head of a valley through two gateways and over three cattle grids. Just beyond the third, go through a metal gate to the right and over the bridge.

⑥ Go ahead then bear left to another gate and follow the track uphill and left to a wall. Turn right at the end of the wall along a lane between stone walls. Continue along the track to a gate and cross a footbridge.

⑦ Turn right through a gate and follow the track uphill, passing through another gate. Turn left at another track, making towards the farmhouse, but bear right across the grass to meet a metalled lane. Turn right and follow the lane over a cattle grid.

⑧ 100yds (91m) beyond the farm on the right, turn left up a signed footpath. After a cattle grid turn right and follow the track, passing through a gate. At **Coldstonefold Farm** turn right and follow the track uphill through three gates on to a metalled lane. Turn left and go uphill to meet the main road. Turn right to return to the **Miners Arms**.

WHERE TO EAT AND DRINK ℹ

The **Miners Arms** in Greenhow offers meals and bar snacks, as well as good local beer. **Stump Cross Caverns** has a tea room. Pateley Bridge is well served with hotels, pubs, restaurants and tea rooms. **Apothecary's House** serves light lunches and teas. **Grassfields Country House Hotel** in Low Wath Road has both a restaurant and a bistro in an elegant Georgian mansion.

WHAT TO LOOK FOR ℹ

Although limestone is the bedrock of the upper part of Greenhow Hill, in the valleys to the east it is the characteristic **millstone grit** that forms the landscape. A carboniferous sandstone, millstone grit is the typical local building material, and most of Greenhow village's houses are made from it. You can recognise it by the large, shiny grains of quartz embedded in it. It's a very hard stone, so, unlike limestone, does not carve easily; fine detail is not something you would expect on a millstone grit building. As its name suggests, however, its hardness made it ideal for millstones. Nidderdale Marble, a dark, metamorphosed limestone that takes a high polish, was quarried in the area, too. It was used in local churches – including Fountains Abbey – for thin decorative columns.

Around Reeth in the Heart of Swaledale

Farmers, miners, knitters and nuns all played their part in the history of this part of Swaledale.

•DISTANCE•	5½ miles (9km)
•MINIMUM TIME•	2hrs
•ASCENT / GRADIENT•	508ft (155m) ▲▲▲
•LEVEL OF DIFFICULTY•	🚶 🚶 🚶
•PATHS•	Field and riverside paths, lanes and woodland, 14 stiles
•LANDSCAPE•	Junction of Swaledale and Arkengarthdale, with field and surrounding moorland
•SUGGESTED MAP•	aqua3 OS Outdoor Leisure 30 Yorkshire Dales – Northern & Central
•START / FINISH•	Grid reference: SE 039993
•DOG FRIENDLINESS•	Dogs should be on leads for majority of walk
•PARKING•	In Reeth, behind fire station, or by the Green
•PUBLIC TOILETS•	Reeth, near Buck Hotel

BACKGROUND TO THE WALK

Reeth has always had a strategic role in the Yorkshire Dales. Set above the junction of Swaledale and Arkengarthdale on Mount Calva, it controlled the important route westwards from Richmond. Sheep were, for a long time, the basis of Reeth's prosperity – it has been a market town since 1695 – and there are still annual sheep sales each autumn, as well as the important Reeth Show around the beginning of September. The wool was used in Reeth's important knitting industry– both the men and women would click away with their needles at stockings and other garments. Reeth also used to be a centre for the lead mining industry, which extended up Arkengarthdale and over Marrick Moor.

Two Bridges and a Church

Reeth Bridge, reached by the Leyburn road from the Green, has suffered over the years from the effects of the swollen River Swale. The present bridge dates from the early 18th century, replacing one washed away in 1701, itself built after its predecessor succumbed in 1547. The path beside the river takes us to Grinton Bridge. Nearby is Grinton church, once the centre of a huge parish that took in the whole of Swaledale, making very long journeys necessary for marriages and funerals. Curiously, it began life as a mission church for the Augustinian Canons of far-away Bridlington Priory on the east coast.

Nuns and Schools at Marrick

The approach to Marrick Priory along the lane suggests that you are about to reach one of the most important churches in the Dales. In a way that is true. Marrick in the Middle Ages was home to a group of Benedictine Nuns. It was founded by Roger de Aske, whose descendent, Robert, was one of the leaders of the Pilgrimage of Grace, the uprising against King Henry VIII's closure of the monasteries. Hilda Prescott's novel *The Man on a Donkey,*

Walk 33

about Robert Aske and the Pilgrimage, is partly set at Marrick. Today the nuns' buildings are partly demolished or absorbed into farm buildings. The church was reduced in size in 1811, and the complex is now used as a Youth Centre for the Diocese of Ripon and Leeds, offering outdoor sports and adventure training. After Marrick Priory the path climbs steeply uphill on rough stone steps called the Nun's Causey (a corruption of causeway). Now used as part of the Coast to Coast Walk, from St Bee's Head in Cumbria to Robin Hood's Bay on the east coast, this is said to be the route which the nuns from the Priory built so they could reach the old Richmond road that ran along the summit of the hill. The original 365 steps have been broken up and removed over the centuries, but the path still retains a suitably medieval atmosphere.

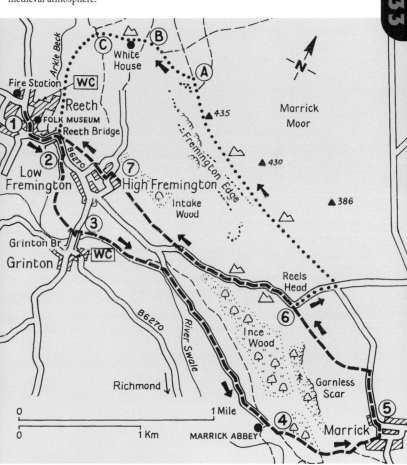

Walk 33 Directions

① From the **Green**, walk downhill, in the direction of Leyburn, to **Reeth Bridge**. Over the bridge, continue along the road as it swings right. About 100yds (91m) along,

turn right at a footpath sign to **Grinton Bridge**.

② Follow the path through a gate and across fields to ascend steps and through a gate on to the bridge. Turn left, cross the road and take a track beside the bridge.

Walk 33

③ Follow the riverside path over four stiles, on to a metalled lane. Turn right and follow the lane to **Marrick Priory**. Walk past the buildings, over a cattle grid, and turn left through a gate signed 'Marrick'.

④ Walk up the grassy track, through a wooden gate and up the paved path through woodland. Go through a gate, up the path and through three more gates. Opposite **Harlands House** turn left up the metalled road, and left again at the T-junction.

⑤ Follow the road for ¼ mile (400m), and turn left over a stile at a footpath sign. Walk up the field, going right over a waymarked, gated stile and follow the wall, to go over another gated stile. Continue over a further stile by a metal gate, then through a second metal gate on to a road.

⑥ Turn left and follow the road for ¾ mile (1.2km). Where the road bends left, turn right through a stile signed 'Fremington'. Follow the path through fields, going through a gate, to another stile, then along a path to a lane.

⑦ Turn left. At the houses turn right, and as the lane bends left, go ahead to a stile by a gate. Keep by the wall on the left, and follow the path through four stiles back to **Reeth Bridge**. Cross the bridge and follow the road back to the **Green**.

From Reeth up to Fremington Edge

For wide views of Swaledale and Arkengarthdale, take this extra section,
which takes you up on to Fremington Edge.
See map and information panel for Walk 33

•DISTANCE•	7 miles (11.3km)
•MINIMUM TIME•	3hrs
•ASCENT / GRADIENT•	328ft (100m) ▲▲▲
•LEVEL OF DIFFICULTY•	🚶🚶 🚶

Walk 34 Directions (Walk 33 option)

You can extend your walk in the heart of Swaledale by climbing up to the crags of Fremington Edge.

At Point ⑥ on the main walk turn right, uphill. By the road sign to **Marrick**, go left through a gap stile. Follow the track uphill, going over a stile beside a metal gate, and climb to reach spoil heaps. You are now on **Fremington Edge**, with its superb views across the dale towards **Reeth**.

You will see the dry-stone walls all around you, some of them reaching in long, straight lines to the summit of the moors. These were the result of the enclosure of land after the Parliamentary Enclosure Act of 1778. Such enclosure was recommended by Sir Thomas Elliot of Fremington, who was responsible for the improvement of much of Yorkshire's moorland. Look for a gate in the wall to the left just beyond the spoil heaps, Point Ⓐ.

Go through the gate and half right.

Walk through a gap in a wall and down towards **White House**. You are passing through the remains of chert mines. Chert, a hard black or white stone rather like flint, was used, finely ground, in the pottery industry. You will reach a track by a footpath sign, Point Ⓑ. Cross the track and go along the grassy track to pass behind White House. Go through a gated stile and follow the path between two hummocks. The path descends to a track, Point Ⓒ.

Cross this track and go over a stile, past a barn and through two more stiles. Bend left to walk along a ridge parallel with the river, with a wall on your left. Go through a gated stile, then through a squeeze stile to the left of two iron gates in a crossing wall. Follow the path to a gated stile on to **Reeth Bridge**, rejoining the main walk. Cross the bridge to return to the **Green**.

WHERE TO EAT AND DRINK ⓘ
All three of Reeth's pubs – The **King's Arms** and the **Black Bull** (next door to each other) and the **Buck Inn** – provide good food at lunchtime and in the evenings. The Black Bull is particularly noted for its pies. There are also tea rooms and cafés around the Green.

Walk 35

River and Woodland at Bolton Abbey

Over moorland and alongside the Strid to the ruined priory.

•DISTANCE•	6¾ miles (10.8km)
•MINIMUM TIME•	2hrs 30min
•ASCENT / GRADIENT•	870ft (265m) ▲ ▲ ▲
•LEVEL OF DIFFICULTY•	👫 👫 👫
•PATHS•	Field and moorland paths, then level riverside paths, 3 stiles
•LANDSCAPE•	Moorland with wide views and riverside woodland
•SUGGESTED MAP•	aqua3 OS Outdoor Leisure 2 Yorkshire Dales – Southern & Western
•START / FINISH•	Grid reference: SE 071539
•DOG FRIENDLINESS•	Must be on lead in woodland and on moorland
•PARKING•	Main car park at Bolton Abbey
•PUBLIC TOILETS•	By car park and at Cavendish Pavilion

Walk 35 Directions

Leave the car park past the **Village Store** and the telephone box. Turn right, walk down the left side of the green, then turn left. Pass under the arch, an aquaduct built in the 18th century to carry water to a mill, to reach the battlemented **Bolton Hall**, originally the gateway to Bolton Priory (it was never an abbey), and later a hunting lodge for the Earls of Cumberland and their successors the Dukes of Devonshire, who still own the estate.

Opposite the Hall turn left on to a track, through a signed gate. At the top of the track, go through a gate on the right, with a bridleway sign. Walk half left to pass the corner of the pools, and on through the gate beyond. After the gate, turn right towards another gate into the wood. Follow the signed track through the wood to another gate out into a field. Follow the blue waymarks across the fields, to ascend a small hill, from which there are excellent views west towards the **Aire Valley** and north over **Barden Fell**. Descend to a gate, and 20yds (18m) beyond, take a path downhill to the right to a gated stone stile on to the road. Turn right along the road. After 200yds (183m) go right through a gate by a sign '**FP to B6160**'. Follow the path across the fields, going over a stile, to reach a wall. Turn right, following the wall and then the waymarked posts, descending to a stile on to the road.

WHILE YOU'RE THERE ⓘ

Take a trip on the **Embsay and Bolton Abbey Steam Railway**, which has a station 1½ miles (2.4km) south of the Priory. Operated by enthusiasts, the railway runs steam trains at weekends, and on most days in August; at other times there is a historic diesel service. At Christmas and on other special days there are themed rides, and the railway also holds regular Thomas the Tank Engine Days.

Walk 35

Turn left and walk along the road for 300yds (274m), then turn right into a car park and pass beside the **Strid Woods Nature Trails** kiosk. Here you can learn about the birds and plants of the Strid Woods, which are freely open to the public and well way-marked. Follow woodland paths down to the riverbank, signposted to **the Strid**. Here, the **River Wharfe** thunders through a narrow gorge between rocks, the Strid itself. This was a place loved by the Victorians, but the flow is fast and the river is 30ft (9m) deep, so don't be tempted to cross; there have been many drownings here over the years. From the Strid, continue to follow the easy riverside path until you reach an information board and gateway near the **Cavendish Pavilion café**. A survivor from the first years of the 20th century, the Pavilion, which has been restored and added to over the years, is still reminiscent of leisurely sunny days in the 1920s.

Go through the gate, turn left by the café and go over the footbridge. Turn right immediately at the end, signed '**Bolton Abbey**'. Follow the footpath parallel with the river, to descend to a bridge beside stepping stones over the river by the **Priory**. This was built for Augustinian Canons who founded their house here in 1154. The ruins make one of the most romantic scenes in the country, and all the great English artists, from Girtin and Turner on, have painted it. Much of what remains was complete by 1220; the last prior, unaware of the coming storm that would sweep away monastic life, began a tower at the west end. It remained unfinished when the monasteries were suppressed. Most of the buildings fell gradually into ruin, but the nave of the Priory church was given to the local people, and it is still their parish church. Cross the bridge and walk straight ahead up the slope and the steps to a gateway – known locally as the **Hole in the Wall**. Go through the gateway then straight ahead beside the green to reach the car park.

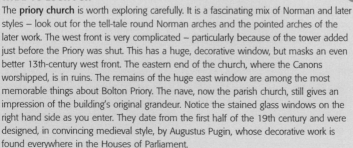

Walk 36

Scar House and Nidderdale

A walk in Upper Nidderdale, with natural and artificial landscapes.

•DISTANCE•	8¼ miles (13.3km)
•MINIMUM TIME•	3hrs 30min
•ASCENT / GRADIENT•	886ft (270m) ▲▲▲
•LEVEL OF DIFFICULTY•	🚶 🚶 🚶
•PATHS•	Moorland tracks, field paths and lanes, 16 stiles
•LANDSCAPE•	High hills of Upper Nidderdale, farmland and riverside
•SUGGESTED MAP•	aqua3 OS Explorer 298 Nidderdale or OS Outdoor Leisure 30 Yorkshire Dales – Northern & Central
•START / FINISH•	Grid reference: SE 070766
•DOG FRIENDLINESS•	Can be off leads on moorland, on lead in farmland
•PARKING•	Signed car park at top of reservoir access road
•PUBLIC TOILETS•	By car park

BACKGROUND TO THE WALK

Opened in 1936, Scar House is one of a string of reservoirs in Nidderdale that serve the city of Bradford, 30 miles (48km) to the south – the others include Angram, to the west, and Gouthwaite, down the valley towards Pateley Bridge. It is still possible to see evidence around the dam of the remains of the village in which the navvies who built it lived and of the ancillary buildings where they stored machinery and dressed the stone. There were some protests before the dams were built about the drowning of parts of the valley, and rumours that Nidderdale was left out of the Yorkshire Dales National Park when it was designated in 1954 because the reservoirs had blighted the landscape. Redress was made in 1994 when 603 square miles (1562 sq km) of Nidderdale became an Area of Outstanding Natural Beauty.

How Stean Gorge

'Yorkshire's Little Switzerland' says the publicity for How Stean Gorge. The How Stean Beck has forced its way through the limestone here, cutting a gorge up to 80ft (25m) deep, with pools and overhangs enough to please both geologists and small children. Lichen and moss cling to the rock walls, and trees overhang it precariously. For a fee, you can enter the gorge, crossing and re-crossing by footbridges and exploring the narrow paths. The more adventurous can borrow a torch to investigate the deep Tom Taylor's Cave, said to be named after a highwayman who holed up here.

The village of Middlesmoor, visible after passing How Stean Gorge, is one of the most dramatically-sited in the area. Set high on a bluff of the hills overlooking the Nidd Valley, its 19th-century church is on the site of a building thought to have been founded by St Chad; it contains the head of a Saxon Cross. One of the most notorious of Victorian murderers, Eugene Aram, who killed his wife's lover and was hanged when the body came to light 14 years later, was married here. Following the Nidderdale Way from Lofthouse, you may well see groups donning caving gear. They are likely to be preparing to enter the Goyden Pot system, 3½ miles (5.8km) of underground caves and passages cut through the limestone by the River Nidd. An early guide book noted that 'Goyden Pot Hole is a large Rock, into which the River Nidd enters by an arch finely formed… with a lighted candle a person may walk three hundred yards into it with safety.' This procedure is not recommended today! Goyden Pot connects with Manchester Hole, a little further upstream, where the river may also disappear; the riverbed above is frequently dry.

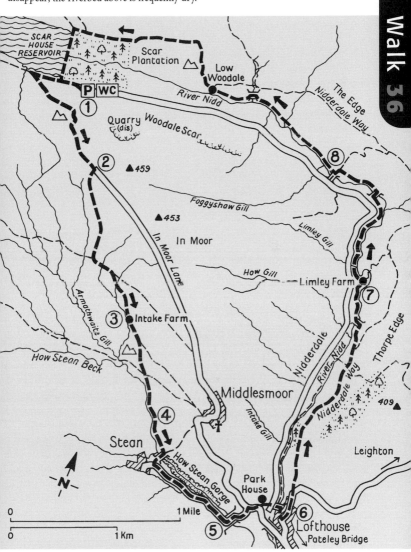

Walk 36 Directions

① Walk towards the dam wall and continue along the left side of the reservoir to a **Nidderdale Way** signpost, just before a gate. Follow the track left uphill. The track levels and goes through a gate. A few paces beyond, go right through a gate in the wall.

② Go diagonally towards the wall on your right, then follow a faint path it as it bends left. At a track turn left, go over two cattle grids

Walk 36

and turn right through the field towards a gate in a crossing hedge. Walk down the next field and pass between farm buildings, following the waymark, to a gate.

③ Cross the field to a handgate by the barn. Pass to the right of a wall to reach a wooden stile. Continue through woodland, ascending left to a waymark, then along the hillside to a stile, where you descend to the riverside path.

④ Go through a squeeze stile, and where the path divides take the left-hand fork, away from the wire fence. Ascend to a ladder stile, then to a stone stile by a **Nidderdale Way** sign. Turn right, go through a gate and cross a footbridge. Ascend the steps to two more stiles on to a lane. Turn left down the lane, passing **How Stean Gorge** entrance, to a stone bridge.

> **WHERE TO EAT AND DRINK** ⓘ
>
> The **Crown Hotel** in Lofthouse does substantial bar meals at lunchtime and in the evenings, and serves good Yorkshire beer. The **How Stean Gorge café** has a very good local reputation and an extensive menu; the raspberry pavlova is a special favourite!

⑤ Go left over the bridge, and turn right at the T-junction, signed 'Lofthouse'. Where the road bends right, go ahead to a gate and to the right of the buildings. Go through another gate, across the road and ahead over the bridge. Turn right and pass between buildings to reach the village street.

⑥ Turn left and climb the hill. As the road bends right, go left down a grassy track to a gate. Continue along the lower track through four gates, then follow the waymarks to

> **WHAT TO LOOK FOR** ⓘ
>
> The **red kite**, once a familiar sight all over England, was hunted almost to extinction in the 19th century. It has now been reintroduced in Yorkshire, and the birds have been seen over-wintering in Upper Nidderdale. They have flown in from their nesting sites on the Harewood Estate, near Leeds, or from Scotland. Their long, angled wings and translucent forked tails make them distinctive. Mature birds have rusty-red plumage, with white feathers around the head.

the river bank. Cross the river to another gate, and continue along the bank, over two stiles to a gate. Turn right towards the farm.

⑦ Just after the first buildings on your left, go through a gateway, through another gate and on to a riverside path. Follow the path over two stiles to a footbridge with a stile at its end. Cross over and turn left to continue along the riverside, going through a gate and over a stile to reach a gate on to a track.

⑧ Turn left over the cattle grid, then right just before a bridge. Where the track bends right, go ahead through four stiles to a gate. Cross a stream to another gate and follow the fence down to a field. Go through a waymarked gate to pass between buildings to another gate. The track climbs right and goes through five gates, turning towards the dam and descending to a track. Turn right and go through a gate. The track becomes metalled. Cross the dam back to the car park.

> **WHILE YOU'RE THERE** ⓘ
>
> Nidderdale is highly regarded for its fishing. If you want to fish in Scar House reservoir – mainly for trout and grayling – you can obtain a ticket from the post offices in Lofthouse or Pateley Bridge.

Villages, Falls and Intriguing Follies

From West Burton to Aysgarth and back, via the famous Aysgarth Falls and some unusual farm buildings.

Walk 37

•DISTANCE•	4 miles (6.4km)
•MINIMUM TIME•	1hr 30min
•ASCENT / GRADIENT•	394ft (120m)
•LEVEL OF DIFFICULTY•	
•PATHS•	Field and riverside paths and tracks, 35 stiles
•LANDSCAPE•	Two typical dales villages, fields and falls on the River Ure
•SUGGESTED MAP•	aqua3 OS Outdoor Leisure 30 Yorkshire Dales – Northern & Central
•START / FINISH•	Grid reference: SE 017867
•DOG FRIENDLINESS•	Dogs should be on leads
•PARKING•	Centre of West Burton, by (but not on) the Green
•PUBLIC TOILETS•	None on route; Aysgarth National Park visitor centre is close

BACKGROUND TO THE WALK

Many people regard West Burton as the prettiest village in the Dales. Its wide, irregular green, with a fat obelisk of 1820, is surrounded by small stone cottages, formerly homes to the quarrymen and miners of the district – but no church. Villagers had to make the trek to Aysgarth for services. West Burton has always been an important centre. It is at the entrance to Bishopdale, with its road link to Wharfedale. South is the road to Walden Head, now a dead end for motorists, but for walkers an alternative route to Starbotton and Kettlewell. At the end of the walk you'll travel for a short time, near Flanders Hall, along Morpeth Gate, the old packhorse route to Middleham.

Two Halves of Aysgarth

After crossing the wide flood plain of Bishopdale Beck, and crossing Eshington Bridge, you climb across the hill to descend into Aysgarth. A village of two halves, the larger part, which you come to first, is set along the main A684 road. The walk takes you along the traditional field path from this part of the village to its other half, set around St Andrew's Church. It's worth looking inside; it contains the spectacular choir screen brought here from Jervaulx Abbey, down the dale, when it was closed by Henry VIII. Like the elaborate stall beside it, it was carved by the renowned Ripon workshops.

The Falls and the Wood

Beyond the church, the path follows the river beside Aysgarth's Middle and Lower Falls. The Falls were formed by the Ure eating away at the underlying limestone as it descends from Upper Wensleydale to join the deeper Bishopdale. They are now one of the most popular tourist sights in the Yorkshire Dales National Park and the Upper Falls, by the bridge, featured in the film *Robin Hood, Prince of Thieves*. Robin (Kevin Costner) fought Little John here with long staves.

Mrs Sykes' Follies

On the return leg of the walk, you pass two oddities in the parkland behind the house at Sorrellsykes Park. These two follies were built in the 18th century by Mrs Sykes and no one seems to knows why. One is a round tower, with a narrowing waist like a diabolo. The other, sitting like Thunderbird 3 ready for lift-off, is known to local people as the 'Rocket Ship'. It is of no practical use, except for minimal shelter in the square room in its base, but it is just one of many folly cones throughout Britain. None of the others, however, have this elaborate arrangement of fins – presumably added because the builder had doubts about its stability.

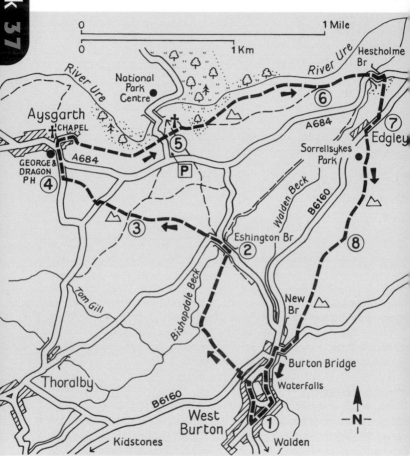

Walk 37 Directions

① Leave the **Green** near the Village Shop. Opposite '**Meadowcroft**' go left, signed '**Eshington Bridge**'. Cross the road, turn right then left, through a gate and down steps. Pass the barn, go through a gateway and across the field. Go through a gap

in the wall with a stile beyond, then bend right to a stile on to the road.

② Turn left, go over the bridge and ahead up the narrow lane. As it bends left go ahead through a stile, signed '**Aysgarth**', then on through a gated stile. Go ahead to a gap in the fence near a barn, then through a gate. Bend left to a gate in the

> **WHERE TO EAT AND DRINK** ⓘ
> In Aysgarth the **George and Dragon** is a good family pub serving meals. Up the road from the church, just off the route of the walk, **Palmer Flatt Hotel** has bar meals and a restaurant, as well as a beer garden with distant views. In West Burton, the **Fox and Hounds** is a traditional village pub serving meals. **Aysgarth Falls National Park Centre**, across the river from the church, has a good coffee shop.

field corner, go through a gateway and on to a stile. Turn right and descend to a signpost.

③ Go ahead to a stile in the field corner. Follow the signpost uphill to a gateway and go through a stile on the right. Cross the field half left to go through a gated stile on to a lane. Turn left, then almost immediately right through a stile, signed '**Aysgarth**'. Go through three stiles to a road.

④ Turn right into the village, past the **George and Dragon**. At the left bend, go ahead toward the chapel, then right at the green, and follow the lane. Go through a stile by **Field House** and to another stile, turning left along the track. Follow the path through eight stiles to the road.

⑤ Go ahead into the churchyard, pass right of the church and go through two stiles, through woodland, then over another stile.

> **WHILE YOU'RE THERE** ⓘ
> Visit the **Yorkshire Carriage Museum** by the bridge below the church in Aysgarth. Housed in a former cotton mill that wove cloth for Garibaldi's 'Red Shirts', the revolutionary army of 19th-century Italy, the museum has a fascinating display of old-time transport, from carriages and carts to hearses and fire engines.

Follow the path downhill towards the river, descending steps to a gate, then a stile. When the footpath reaches the river bank, take a signed stile right.

⑥ Follow the path over two stiles to a signpost, bending right across the field to a road. Turn left over the bridge, turning right into woodland a few paces beyond, signed '**Edgley**'. Go over a stile and cross the field to a gate on to the road.

⑦ Turn right. About 150yds (137m) along, go left over a stile, signed '**Flanders Hall**'. Walk below the follies on the ridge to a footpath sign, cross a track and go uphill to a stile with steps to it.

⑧ Opposite a stone barn go right, through a gate, and go downhill through two more gates, then over three stiles to a lane. Turn right and go over a bridge to join the village road. Turn left, back to the **Green**.

> **WHAT TO LOOK FOR** ⓘ
> The woods around Aysgarth have long been used for the production of hazel poles, and there is evidence of this trade on the walk, with the now-overgrown stumps of the hazel trees sprouting many branches, some of them of considerable age. In Freeholders' Wood beside the Middle and Lower Falls, on the opposite side of the River Ure from the route of the walk, the National Park Authority has restarted this ancient craft of coppicing. The name comes from the French *couper*, meaning to cut. Each year the hazel trees are cut back to a stump – called a stool – from which new shoots are allowed to grow. As long as they are protected from grazing cattle, the shoots develop into poles, and can be harvested after around seven years' growth. Hazel poles are traditionally used for making woven hurdles, and the thinner stems for basket-weaving.

Dalesfolk Traditions in Hubberholme

From JB Priestley's favourite Dales village, along Langstrothdale and back via a limestone terrace.

•DISTANCE•	5 miles (8km)
•MINIMUM TIME•	2hrs
•ASCENT / GRADIENT•	394ft (120m) ▲▲▲
•LEVEL OF DIFFICULTY•	🚶🚶 🚶
•PATHS•	Field paths and tracks, steep after Yockenthwaite, 11 stiles
•LANDSCAPE•	Streamside paths and limestone terrace
•SUGGESTED MAP•	aqua3 OS Outdoor Leisure 30 Yorkshire Dales – Northern & Central
•START / FINISH•	Grid reference: SD 927782
•DOG FRIENDLINESS•	Dogs should be on lead, except on section between Yockenthwaite and Cray
•PARKING•	Beside river in village, opposite church (not church parking)
•PUBLIC TOILETS•	None on route

BACKGROUND TO THE WALK

Literary pilgrims visit Hubberholme to see the George Inn, where JB Priestley could often be found enjoying the local ale, and the churchyard, the last resting place for his ashes, as he requested. He chose an idyllic spot. Set at the foot of Langstrothdale, Hubberholme is a cluster of old farmhouses and cottages surrounding the church. Norman in origin, St Michael's was once flooded so badly that fish were seen swimming in the nave. One vicar of Hubberholme is said to have carelessly baptised a child Amorous instead of Ambrose, a mistake that, once entered in the parish register, couldn't be altered. Amorous Stanley used his memorable name later in life as part of his stock-in-trade as a hawker.

Church Wood

Hubberholme church's best treasures are of wood. The rood loft above the screen is one of only two surviving in Yorkshire, (the other is at Flamborough, far away on the east coast). Once holding figures of Christ on the Cross, St Mary and St John, it dates from 1558, when such examples of Popery were fast going out of fashion. It still retains some of its once-garish colouring of red, gold and black. Master-carver Robert Thompson provided almost all the rest of the furniture in 1934 – look for his mouse trademark on each piece.

Ancient Yockenthwaite and Remote Cray

Yockenthwaite's name, said to have been derived from an ancient Irish name, Eogan, conjures up images of the ancient past. Norse settlers were here more than 1,000 years ago – and even earlier settlers have left their mark, a Bronze Age stone circle a little further up the valley. The hamlet now consists of a few farm buildings beside the bridge over the Wharfe at the end of Langstrothdale Chase, a Norman hunting ground which used to have its own forest laws and punishments. You walk along a typical Dales limestone terrace to

Walk 38

reach Cray, on the road over from Bishopdale joining Wharfedale to Wensleydale. Here is another huddle of farmhouses, around the White Lion Inn. You then follow the Cray Gill downstream, past a series of small cascades. For a more spectacular waterfall, head up the road from the inn a little way to Cray High Bridge.

Burning the Candle

Back in Hubberholme, the George Inn was once the vicarage. It is the scene each New Year's Day of an ancient auction. It begins with the lighting of a candle, after which the auctioneer asks for bids for the year's tenancy of the 'Poor Pasture', a 16 acre (7.2ha) field behind the inn. All bids have to be completed before the candle burns out. In the days when the George housed the vicar, he ran the auction. Today a local auctioneer takes the role, and a merry time is had by all. The proceeds from the auction go to help the old people of the village.

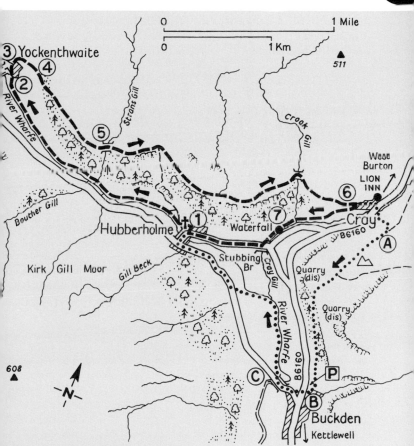

Walk 38 Directions

① Go through a **Dales Way** signed gate near the east end of the church, bend left and then take the lower path, signed '**Yockenthwaite**'. Walk beside the river for 1¼ miles (2km) through three stiles, a gate and two more stiles. The path eventually rises to another stone stile into **Yockenthwaite**.

Walk 38

② Go through the stile and bend left to a wooden gate. Continue through a farm gate by a sign to **Deepdale and Beckermonds**. Before the track reaches a bridge go right and swing round to a sign to **Cray and Hubberholme**.

③ Go up the hill and, as the track curves right, continue to follow the **Cray and Hubberholme** sign. Part-way up the hill go right at a footpath sign through a wooden gate in a fence.

④ Go through a second gate to a footpath sign and ascend the hillside. Go through a gap in a wall by another signpost and follow the obvious path through several gaps in crossing walls. Go over two stone stiles and ascend again to a footbridge between stiles.

⑤ Cross the bridge and continue through woodland to another stile. Wind round the head of the valley and follow the signpost to **Cray**.

Go over a footbridge. The footpath winds its way down the valley side. Go through a gate and straight ahead across meadow land to a gateway on to a track, and on to a stone barn.

⑥ Bend to the right beyond the barn, down to a public footpath sign to **Stubbing Bridge**. Go down the path between stone walls and through a wooden gate and on to the grassy hillside. Pass another footpath sign and continue downhill to meet the stream by a waterfall.

⑦ Continue along the streamside path through woodland. Go over a wooden stile and on past a barn to a stone stile on to the road. Turn right along the road back to the parking place in **Hubberholme**.

WHILE YOU'RE THERE ℹ️

If you've the energy, a walk to the summit of nearby **Buckden Pike** will reward you with fine views and a memorial to five Polish airmen whose plane crashed there in November 1942. One man survived the crash, following a fox's footprints through the snow down to safety at a farm. The cross he erected has a fox's head set in the base as thanksgiving. Buckden Pike is best climbed up the track called Walden Road from Starbotton.

WHAT TO LOOK FOR ℹ️

A number of barns in the area have been converted to become holiday accommodation **bunk barns**. An initiative set up by the Yorkshire Dales National Park Authority and the Countryside Commission in 1979, the aim is to solve two problems – how to preserve the now-redundant barns that are so vital a part of the Dales landscape, and a lack of simple accommodation for walkers. Also known as stone tents, these bunkhouse barns offer farmers an alternative to letting the barns decay. They add basic amenities for cooking, washing and sleeping (and sometimes extras like comfortable chairs!) and let them to families or groups at a realistic nightly rate. They help to keep the farms viable, and both walkers and farmers benefit in other ways, too; meeting each other helps each to appreciate the needs and hopes of the other. As one farmer's wife said, 'We've made a lot of friends though the barn'.

Down the Dale from Cray to Buckden

Take this additional loop that goes via a Roman road to Buckden, and back to Hubberholme along the riverside.
See map and information panel for Walk 38

•DISTANCE•	7¾ miles (12.5km)
•MINIMUM TIME•	3hrs
•ASCENT / GRADIENT•	623ft (190m) ▲▲▲
•LEVEL OF DIFFICULTY•	🚶🚶🚶

Walk 39 **Directions** (Walk 38 option)

You can see more of the beautiful Upper Wharfedale scenery by extending Walk 38 from Cray to the peaceful village of Buckden.

At Point ⑥ on the main walk, continue straight ahead along the track and wind between the farm buildings to reach a metalled road by the **White Lion Inn**.

Cross the road and go over the stepping stones, then pass through a gate. Go straight ahead uphill to a signpost, and bend left, following a wall. At the top of the hill follow the wall as it diverts right to a gate, just beyond which is a signpost to **Buckden**, Point Ⓐ.

Turn right along the path, which bends right; go over a stile and then through a gate by a large boulder. You are now on **Buckden Rake**, possibly the remains of a Roman road built by the army of Julius Agricola to link the fort at Ilkley in Wharfedale (possibly the Roman outpost of Olicana) to Virosidum

(Bainbridge in Wensleydale). The grassy path becomes a stony track and goes downhill through a wooden gate and into woodland.

Descend into **Buckden car park** and go straight ahead by the 'No Exit' sign on to the main road by the Buckden Village Restaurant, Point Ⓑ.

Buckden, always a strategically important point in the Dales, is an attractive estate village at the junction of several roads and tracks. It was a centre from which the Norman and medieval noblemen set out to hunt deer in the Langstrothdale Forest; the Buck Inn is a reminder of this tradition. The village is dominated by Buckden Pike, 2,304ft (702m) high, to the north east. Cross the road and follow the track beside **the Green**. Turn right along the road and over the bridge. A few paces beyond go over a gated stile on the right, signed '**Hubberholme**', Point Ⓒ. Go over three wooden stiles, and eventually swing away from the riverside to reach a road. Turn right back to **Hubberholme**, turning right over the bridge back to the church and the car parking place.

The Lead Mines at Old Gang

Ruined buildings give eloquent testimony to Swaledale's important industrial past.

•DISTANCE•	7¾ miles (12.5km)
•MINIMUM TIME•	3hrs
•ASCENT / GRADIENT•	853ft (260m)
•LEVEL OF DIFFICULTY•	
•PATHS•	Tracks and moorland paths – a little road walking at end
•LANDSCAPE•	Pasture and moorland
•SUGGESTED MAP•	aqua3 OS Outdoor Leisure 30 Yorkshire Dales – Northern & Central
•START / FINISH•	Grid reference: SD 989999
•DOG FRIENDLINESS•	Can be off lead except near sheep
•PARKING•	At junction of two minor roads, in valley of Old Gang Beck
•PUBLIC TOILETS•	None on route

Walk 40 Directions

From the bridge over the beck, turn up the track that goes upstream by the 'Bridleway only, no vehicles' sign. Follow the track for a mile to reach **Old Gang Smelting Mills**.

The area around Old Gang was one of the most intensively-mined parts of Swaledale in the 18th and 19th centuries. The lead-bearing veins here were very complex, so there are many – and confusing – remains all around you. The largest surviving building beside the track at Old Gang is the smelting mill, while on the hillside behind you can see the columns of stone that were the peat house. This open-sided building was 390ft (119m) long and 21ft (6.4m) wide, and originally had a thatched roof. It could hold enough locally-dug peat for a year's smelting. On the hillside between the mill and the peat house is the entrance to Hard Level, opened in 1785. Continue along the track for another ¾ mile (1.2km), going right where the path forks, following the **Level House Bridge** sign. Level House, which stood at the junction of the paths, was a dwelling built in the late 17th century for one of the partners in the early mining here. You will see the remains of the rails that took the ore-laden trucks from the mines to the smelting mills along the way.

At the bridge, go through a gate, cross the bridge and go uphill. This track follows the Old Rake Vein,

---

WHILE YOU'RE THERE

Further your knowledge of the district's lead mining by visiting **Gunnerside**. The valley of Gunnerside Gill, which stretched north from the village, was one of the most heavily-mined areas in Swaledale. A stroll up the valley will enable you to see mine entrances and the remains of crushing mills. There is a particularly impressive show at the Bunton site, where the valley is steep, while beyond are the ruins of the Blakethwaite Smelting Mill.

Walk 40

towards the **Merryfield Mines**. Where a track comes in from the left, turn right, following a path down into the valley to cross two streams, past spoil heaps and some small cairns. When you reach a fence, continue ahead with the fence on your right. At a gate in the fence, go through and continue with the fence on your left. On reaching a stony area, turn right to follow a stream valley. Cross a small stream and continue ahead along the track. Go through an area of spoil heaps and shafts, bending right through a bare rocky area to continue along a grassy track, through more heaps.

There are views into **Arkengarthdale**, another heavily mined area, to the right, and you can see the remains of hushes. These were an early method of reaching the ore. At the top of a steep slope a stream was dammed with turf. Once enough water had collected, the dam was breached and the water rushing downhill gouged a trench in the slope, with luck exposing the vein.

Where another track comes in from the right go left and follow the track to a road. Turn right and follow the road, which crosses a cattle grid. Go over a footbridge beside the ford at **Fore Gill Gate** (viewers of BBC television's *All Creatures Great and*

Small series will recognise this as the ford crossed in the opening titles by the vet's car) and ascend the hill, then continue downhill.

Before reaching the bridge over the **Old Gang Beck**, you will cross the horizontal flue from the old **Surrender Smelt Mill**, downstream to your left.

The flue was connected to the chimney up on the hill to your right. Such long flues enabled the smelt mills to use higher temperatures to separate the lead from the slag. Some lead vapourises in extreme heat, and this was previously being lost in the atmosphere. The long flues meant that the gases cooled as they went towards the chimney, so the lead solidified in the walls. Men (though it was often boys) could then be sent into the flues to recover the lead deposit. Cross the bridge to return to the parking place.

Semerwater – A Legendary Glacial Lake

Legends – perhaps with a basis in dim and distant truth – surround Yorkshire's biggest natural lake.

•DISTANCE•	5 miles (8km)
•MINIMUM TIME•	2hrs
•ASCENT / GRADIENT•	853ft (260m) ▲▲▲
•LEVEL OF DIFFICULTY•	🚶 🚶 🚶
•PATHS•	Field paths and tracks, steep ascent from Marsett, 19 stiles
•LANDSCAPE•	Valley, lake and fine views over Wensleydale
•SUGGESTED MAP•	aqua3 OS Outdoor Leisure 30 Yorkshire Dales – Northern & Central
•START / FINISH•	Grid reference: SD 921875
•DOG FRIENDLINESS•	Dogs should be on leads
•PARKING•	Car park at the north end of the lake
•PUBLIC TOILETS•	None on route

BACKGROUND TO THE WALK

Semerwater was formed as the result of the end of the last Ice Age. Glacial meltwater attempted to drain away down the valley the glacier had gouged out of the limestone, but was prevented from doing so by a wall of boulder clay, dumped by the glacier itself, across the valley's end. So the water built up, forming a lake which once stretched 3 miles (4.8km) up Raydale. Natural silting has gradually filled the upper part of the lake bed, leaving Semerwater – at half a mile (800m) long Yorkshire's largest natural lake.

Legendary Semerwater

Semerwater boasts several legends. One concerns the three huge blocks of limestone deposited by the departing glacier at the water's edge at the north end. Called the Carlow Stone and the Mermaid Stones, they are said to have landed here when the Devil and a giant who lived on Addlebrough, the prominent hill a mile (1.6km) to the east, began lobbing missiles at each other. More famous is the story of the beggar who came to the town that once stood where the lake is now. He went from door to door, asking for food and drink, but was refused by everyone – except the poorest couple. Revealing himself as an angel, he raised his staff over the town, crying 'Semerwater rise, Semerwater sink, And swallow all save this little house, That gave me meat and drink.' The waters overwhelmed the town, leaving the poor people's cottage on the brink of the new lake. Some say the church bells can still be heard ringing beneath the waters.

Behind the Legend

There are indeed the remains of a settlement beneath Semerwater. Houses perched on stilts were built along the water's edge in Iron Age times, though there may have been an earlier settlement here in Neolithic times, too, for flint arrow heads have been found. A Bronze age spear head was found in 1937 when the lake's waters were lowered.

Setts and Quakers

Marsett, at the lake's southern end, and Countersett, to the north, both end with the Old Norse word denoting a place of hill pasture. Marsett is a hamlet of old farmhouses, and on the road to Countersett, at Carr End, is the house where Dr Fothergill was born in 1712. A famous Quaker philanthropist, he founded the Quaker school at Ackworth in South Yorkshire. The American statesman Benjamin Franklin said he found it hard to believe that any better man than Fothergill had ever lived. Countersett has one of several old Friends' Meeting Houses in Wensleydale, and the Hall was home, in the 17th century, to Richard Robinson, who was responsible for the spread of Quakerism in the Dales.

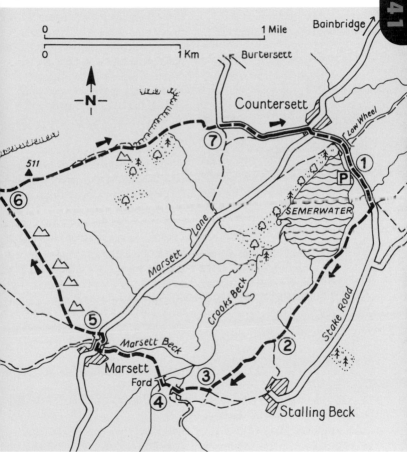

Walk 41 Directions

① Turn right out of the car park up the road. Opposite farm buildings go right over a ladder stile, signed '**Stalling Busk**'. Go through a gated stile and ahead towards the barn, then through two stone stiles. Just beyond the second is a Wildlife Trust sign. Continue over two more stiles to a gate.

② Just beyond the gate, follow the **Marsett** sign to the corner of the field and over a gated stone stile. Follow the waymarked path as it curves beside the river, to a barn.

Walk 41

Go over a stile above the barn to another stile. Cross the field to another stile and on towards another barn, and on further to cross a stream bed.

③ Immediately afterwards, turn right down the well-worn footpath, which curves towards a roofless barn. Cross another three stiles, then turn right, following a path to the trees, with a stone wall on your right. Continue over two stiles to a footbridge and go straight on to a track, where you turn right to reach a ford.

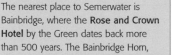

WHAT TO LOOK FOR

Semerwater offers a wide variety of habitats for wildlife. The waters of the lake, which have a high plankton content, support many fish including bream and perch, as well as crayfish. Water birds include great crested grebe and tufted duck. You may also occasionally see Whooper swans. Over the fringes of the lake dragonflies and damsel flies can be seen glittering in the summer. On the wet margins of the lake grow flowers such as marsh marigold, marsh cinquefoil, ragged robin and valerian, while in the dryer areas the wood anemone is frequently found. Birds such as lapwings, redshank and reed bunting may also be seen, while summer visitors include the sandmartin.

④ Before the ford, veer left over a footbridge and back on to the track, which winds into **Marsett**. Just before the village, follow the stream as it goes right, and make for the road by the red telephone box. Turn right over the bridge. 100yds (91m) beyond take a track signed **Burtersett and Hawes** (not the path by the river).

WHILE YOU'RE THERE

Visit **Bainbridge**, with its wide green and attractive houses. The Romans had a fort here, Virosidum, on top of the hill called Brough. The River Bain, crossed by the bridge which gives the village its name, is England's shortest river, running all of 2 miles (3.2km) from Semerwater to the River Ure.

⑤ Walk uphill to a gate on the right at the start of the stone wall. Go over the stile and continue uphill, over three stiles. Soon after the steep path flattens out, you reach a track that crosses the path, coming through a gap in the wall on your left.

⑥ Turn right along the track, which goes through a gate in a wall. Where it divides, take the right fork downhill to a stile. The path descends steeply through two gates, to reach a crossing track. Continue straight ahead and follow the track as it bends left to a gate on to a metalled road.

⑦ Turn right and follow the road downhill to the staggered crossroads, turning right, then left, signed 'Stalling Busk'. Go down the hill, over the bridge and back to the car park.

WHERE TO EAT AND DRINK

The nearest place to Semerwater is Bainbridge, where the **Rose and Crown Hotel** by the Green dates back more than 500 years. The Bainbridge Horn, blown to guide travellers to the village in the dark winter months, hangs here. The hotel serves home-cooked local produce both in the bars and, in the evening, in the Dales Room Restaurant.

A Riverside Circuit High in the Dales

A classic walk in Upper Swaledale from Keld to Muker along Kidsdon Side, and back by the river.

•DISTANCE•	6 miles (9.7km)
•MINIMUM TIME•	2hrs 30min
•ASCENT / GRADIENT•	820ft (250m) ▲ ▲ ▲
•LEVEL OF DIFFICULTY•	🚶 🚶 🚶
•PATHS•	Field and riverside paths and tracks, 10 stiles
•LANDSCAPE•	Hillside and valley, hay meadows, riverside and waterfall
•SUGGESTED MAP•	aqua3 OS Outdoor Leisure 30 Yorkshire Dales – Northern & Central
•START / FINISH•	Grid reference: NY 892012
•DOG FRIENDLINESS•	Dogs on leads (there are lots of sheep)
•PARKING•	Signed car park at west end of village near Park Lodge
•PUBLIC TOILETS•	Keld and Muker

BACKGROUND TO THE WALK

Keld – its name is the Old Norse word for a spring – is one of the most remote of Dales villages. Set at the head of Swaledale, its cluster of grey cottages is a centre for some of the most spectacular walks in North Yorkshire. This walk follows, for part of its way, the traditional route by which the dead of the upper Dales were taken the long distance for burial in Grinton churchyard. Leaving the village, the walk takes the Pennine Way as it follows the sweep of the Swale on its way down to Muker. This is Kisdon Side, on the slopes of the conical hill known as Kisdon. It was formed at the end of the Ice Age; the Swale used to flow west of the hill but glacial debris blocked its course and forced it to the east, in its current bed.

Muker and the mines

As the Pennine Way goes west, eventually to climb the slopes of Great Shunner Fell, the walk joins the Corpse Way and descends into Muker. It is worth taking some time to explore the village. Like many Swaledale settlements, it expanded in the 18th and 19th centuries because of local lead mining. The prominent Literary Institute was built for the mining community; though in a nice reverse of fortunes, when the new chapel came to be built in the 1930s, dressed stone taken from the ore hearths at the Old Gang Mine down the valley was used. The Anglican church, which eventually did away with the long journey to Grinton, dates from 1580.

Rocks and Crackpot

Beyond Muker, the walk passes through hay meadows and along the banks of the Swale. Both sandstone and limestone are found in this section; look out for the sandstone bed underlying the river. The limestone of the area is part of the thick Ten Fathom bed, one of the Yoredale series of sedimentary rocks. Where the valley of Swinner Gill crosses the path are the remains of a small smelt mill which served the nearby Beldi Hill and Swinner Gill Mines. As you ascend the hill beyond, the ruins of Crackpot Hall, a farmhouse long abondoned because of mining subsidence and changes in farming fortune, are to your right. Its name means 'Crows Pothole'.

As the track descends the valley side, the waterfall of Kisdon Force is below you on the Swale, and there are high overhanging crags on the opposite bank. Further along, you turn downhill to the footbridge over the river, beside East Gill Force. Like all the Dales falls, the volume of its water can vary wildly from the merest summer trickle to a raging winter torrent. Whatever its condition, the rocks around can be very slippery and you should take special care if you leave the path to get a better view.

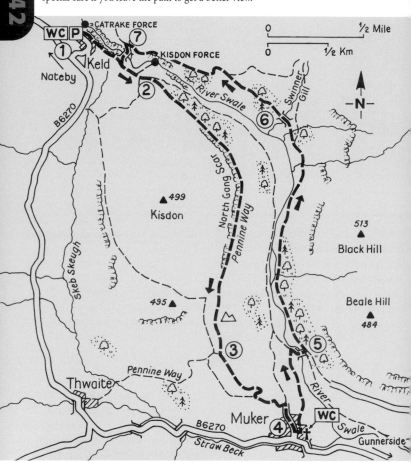

Walk 42 Directions

① Walk back down the car park entrance road, and straight ahead down the gravel track, signed 'Muker'. Continue along at the upper level, ignoring a path

downhill to the left. Go through a gate, pass a sign to **Kisdon Upper Force**, and continue along the track to a signpost.

② Turn right, following the **Pennine Way** National Trail. The path goes through a gated stone

Walk **42**

stile, then through a gap in the wall to continue with a wall on your left. Go on through a gate and over four stiles to descend towards **Muker** to reach a signpost where the **Pennine Way** goes right.

③ Go straight on down the track, marked '**Muker**', between stone walls. Go through a wooden gate, still following the bridleway to **Muker**. The track becomes metalled, as it descends through two gates and into a walled lane in the village to a T-junction.

④ Turn left and left again by a sign to **Gunnerside and Keld**. Follow the paved path through five stiles to reach the river. Turn right and go over a stile to the footbridge.

⑤ Ascend the steps beyond the footbridge and turn left, signed '**Keld**'. Follow the course of the river along a clear track, until it curves right around **Swinner Gill**, over a footbridge by the remains of the lead workings, and through a wooden gate.

⑥ Go straight ahead up the hill and into woodland. The track eventually winds left then right round a stone barn, then downhill through a wooden gate to reach another gate above **Kisdon Force**.

⑦ Go left by a wooden seat, at a sign to **Keld**. Follow the stream down to a footbridge. Go through the gate and turn right, uphill, to a T-junction, where you turn right and follow the path back to the car.

Spectacular Landscapes in Limestone Country

The noble Malham Cove is the majestic highlight of this quintessential limestone Dales walk.

•DISTANCE•	6¼ miles (10km)
•MINIMUM TIME•	3hrs
•ASCENT / GRADIENT•	1,148ft (350m) ▲▲▲
•LEVEL OF DIFFICULTY•	🏃 🏃 🏃
•PATHS•	Well-marked field and moorland paths, more than 400 steps in descent from Malham Cove, 5 stiles
•LANDSCAPE•	Spectacular limestone country, including Malham Cove
•SUGGESTED MAP•	aqua3 OS Outdoor Leisure 30 Yorkshire Dales – Northern & Central
•START / FINISH•	Grid reference: SD 894658
•DOG FRIENDLINESS•	Mostly off lead, except where sheep are present or signs indicate otherwise
•PARKING•	At Water Sinks, near gateway across road
•PUBLIC TOILETS•	Car park in Malham village

BACKGROUND TO THE WALK

As you begin this walk, the stream from Malham Tarn suddenly disappears in a tumble of rocks. This is the aptly-named Water Sinks. In spectacular limestone country like this, it is not unusual for streams to plunge underground – it was subterranean watercourses that sculpted the cave systems beneath your feet. As you will see as you continue, this particular stream has not always been so secretive. The now-dry valley of Watlowes just beyond Water Sinks was formed by water action. It was this stream, in fact, that produced Malham Cove, and once fell over its spectacular cliff in a waterfall 230ft (70m) high. Although in very wet weather the stream goes a little further than Water Sinks, it is 200 years since water reached the cove.

Pavement and Cove

Beyond Watlowes valley you reach a stretch of limestone pavement – not the biggest, but probably the best-known example of this unusual phenomenon in the Dales. The natural fissures in the rock have been enlarged by millennia of rain and frost, forming the characteristic blocks, called clints, and the deep clefts, called grikes. It's worth looking closely into the grikes; their sheltered environment provides a home to spleenworts and ferns, and you will sometimes find rare primulas flowering in their shade. The limestone pavement is the summit of the most spectacular of natural features in the Yorkshire Dales – the huge sweep of the cliffs known as Malham Cove. Take care as you explore the pavement, as the edge is not fenced. As you descend the 400-plus steps, the sheer scale of the Cove becomes apparent; 230ft (70m) high, it was formed by a combination of glacial action, earth movement (it is on the line of the Middle Craven Fault) and the biting away of its lip by the former waterfall.

Walk 43

Fields, Falls and Fairies

On the slopes to the east of Malham Cove you can see ancient terraced fields. Up to 200yds (183m) long, they were painstakingly cut and levelled by Anglian farmers in the 8th century for producing crops. They show how the population was expanding then, and that there was simply not enough farmland on the valley floors to feed everyone. After walking through Malham village, the route passes through fields and a wooded gorge – called Little Gordale – to Janet's Foss. One of the classic waterfalls of the Dales, it is noted for the screen of tufa, a soft, porous limestone curtain formed by deposits from the stream, that now lies over the original lip of stone that was responsible for creating the fall. Janet (or Jennett) was the Queen of the local fairies, and is said to have lived in the cave behind the fall.

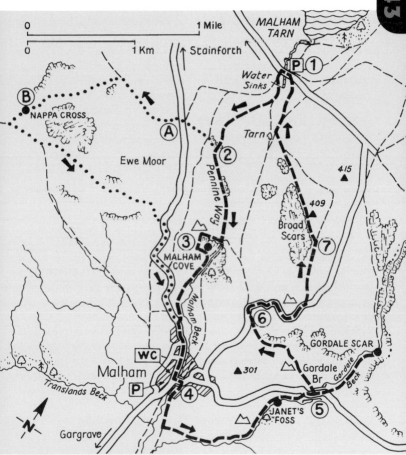

Walk 43 **Directions**

① From the car parking space, walk through the gate, then turn left through the kissing gate at the **Malham Cove** sign. Walk parallel with the dry-stone wall on your left

and follow the dry valley as it bends to reach a stile at the head of another dry valley.

② Turn left and follow the footpath down the valley to reach a stile at the end. Go over the stile, then walk straight ahead to the limestone

Walk 43

pavement at the top of **Malham Cove**. Turn right and walk along the pavement to reach steps. Take greta care here, both of the sheer drop down to your left and the gaps in the limestone pavement (known as grikes). Turn left to cautiously descend more than 400 steps to the foot of the **Cove**.

③ When you reach the bottom turn right along the track beside the river. Go through two kissing gates to reach the road. Turn left and follow the road into the centre of **Malham** village. Turn left to go over the bridge.

④ Turn right along the side of the river on a track, following the signs marked '**Janet's Foss**'. Follow the signposted, mostly gravelled, path through eight gates. Eventually the footpath climbs up through woodland and passes beside the waterfall (Janet's Foss) to a kissing gate. Turn right along the road, towards **Gordale Scar**.

⑤ At the bridge go through a gate to the left. (To visit **Gordale Scar**, continue straight ahead here. Take a signed gate to the left and follow the path up through a field into the gorge. Keep going on the obvious route as far as the waterfall and then follow the same route back to the bridge.) On the main route, follow the signed public footpath uphill through two stiles and out on to a lane.

⑥ Turn right and walk uphill for ¼ mile (400m), to a ladder stile over the wall on your left. Follow the track, going left at a fork to reach another footpath fingerpost.

⑦ Turn left, following the sign, to reach a small tarn. Turn right at the sign for **Malham Tarn**, go over a ladder stile, take the left hand path and follow it back to the car park.

Malham Cove and Nappa Cross

This extra loop on Walk 43 avoids the steep climb down Malham Cove, and adds wide views of the surrounding landscape.
See map and information panel for Walk 43

Walk 44

•DISTANCE•	7½ miles (12km)
•MINIMUM TIME•	3hrs 30min
•ASCENT / GRADIENT•	1,738ft (530m) ▲▲▲
•LEVEL OF DIFFICULTY•	🚶 🚶 🚶

Walk 44 Directions (Walk 43 option)

When you reach the stile at Point ② on Walk 43, turn right up the valley, and go right again over a ladder stile after a few paces. Walk up the field, with a wall on your right, and go over two stiles on to the road by a cattle grid, Point Ⓐ.

Cross the road, go through a gate and follow the stony track uphill. This is an area with evidence, in the form of earthworks, of Iron Age settlements. Off the path to the right is a typical 'shake hole', often seen marked on maps in limestone country. These are usually seen as hollows or deeper depressions in the sheep-cropped turf, formed when caves under the ground, created by the action of streams, have collapsed. Take care not to walk in the dip – shake holes can be dangerous.

Pass through a gap in a wall, then turn half left up a grassy track, past a waymark post. The track passes through three gates until it reaches the stump of **Nappa Cross** in a wall

on the left, Point Ⓑ. The base and restored post of a medieval monastic cross, Nappa Cross is a reminder that vast areas of the upper Dales were owned by the monasteries and supported the huge flocks of sheep that provided the monks' often vast incomes. Just beyond, turn left at a bridleway, signed '**Cove Road**'. This is part of the former packhorse route from Malham down into Ribblesdale. Malham was an important centre for producing zinc ore, which in the late 18th and early 19th centuries was taken to Gargrave for transportation on the Leeds-Liverpool Canal.

Follow the track left through a wall, go past a finger post and descend to a gate on to a road. Turn right, downhill, and follow the road past **Malham Cove** into the village, to rejoin the main walk at Point ④.

Walk 45

The Ascent of Pen-y-ghent

To the summit of one of the Three Peaks, and back by the River Ribble.

•DISTANCE•	6½ miles (10.4km)
•MINIMUM TIME•	3hrs
•ASCENT / GRADIENT•	1,555ft (474m) ▲▲▲
•LEVEL OF DIFFICULTY•	👥 👥 👥
•PATHS•	Easy-to-follow paths and tracks on Pen-y-ghent. Steep descent from summit, farmland paths, 16 stiles
•LANDSCAPE•	One of the Dales' most famous mountains, with spectacular views
•SUGGESTED MAP•	aqua3 OS Outdoor Leisure 2 Yorkshire Dales – Southern & Western
•START / FINISH•	Grid reference: SD 808725
•DOG FRIENDLINESS•	Dogs should be on leads in farmland
•PARKING•	Car park at north end of Horton-in-Ribblesdale
•PUBLIC TOILETS•	At car park

Walk 45 Directions

From the car park, turn right along the road, passing the **Pen-y-ghent Café**. This is the walkers' centre for the area, selling a vast range of books and maps, and running a booking-in and -out service for those walking or climbing in the area. 100yds (91m) beyond, turn left, on to a track, following the **Pennine Way** sign. Go straight on through a hand gate at a junction of paths. The path eventually curves right, towards **Pen-y-ghent**.

Go through a gate and turn right, following the Pen-y-ghent sign. Just

---

WHERE TO EAT AND DRINK ℹ️

The **Pen-y-Ghent Café**, as well as providing all its other services, does good, energy-giving food, specially geared to the needs of walkers. The village's two pubs, the **Crown** and the **Golden Lion** both offer meals and serve good Yorkshire ales.

---

beyond, off the path to the right, is **Hunt Pot**, a gash in the moorland grass that leads into a deep drop beneath. First explored at the end of the 19th century, Hunt Pot has a total descent of 160ft (49m). A little way to the north is Hull Pot, a much larger hole. In wet weather a stream tumbles down its limestone crags into the depths.

Continue over two ladder stiles, climbing steadily and bearing right by a signpost. Keep to the right where the path splits, to reach a stile over a stone wall at the **summit** of the mountain. One of the famous Three Peaks of the Dales (the others, Ingleborough and Whernside are visible from here), Pen-y-ghent's distinctive profile dominates the landscape. Its name, which is Celtic, means either 'the hill on the plain' or 'the windy hill'. Both are appropriate. The ridges that stripe its sides are the result of different rock strata – millstone grit on top, softer shales beneath and,

Walk 45

WHILE YOU'RE THERE

Visit the lively market town of **Settle**, to the south of Horton in Ribblesdale. If you're there on a Tuesday you'll find its market in full swing, in front of the impressive arched Shambles building, with two storeys of shops and homes above them. Up the High Street is a large and ornate 17th-century house called The Folly, and scattered through the town are old houses with carved lintels showing when they were built and their builders' initials.

half way up, a band of limestone. Turn right along the stony path, going downhill. Stay near the wall as the path descends very steeply down the hillside. After the descent you will reach two ladder stiles over a wall on your right. Cross one, following a sign to **Brackenbottom**. As you descend, the limestone quarries that surround **Horton in Ribblesdale** are clearly in view. Although National Park policies are weighted against quarry development, many workings often precede the designation of the Dales as a National Park.

Go over another ladder stile, then two gated stone stiles. At the foot of the hill go over a wooden stile beside a gate by the farm, then through a handgate on to a road. Turn left and follow the road, going straight ahead as another road joins from the left. Take the next turn right to pass a stone barn and reach the main road. Cross and walk down the lane opposite. Before the farm buildings, turn right up a green lane, go over the stepping stones and straight on. Where the wall on the left ends, go left through a gate and down the track. Where the track bends, turn left to go over a bridge and continue straight ahead down the field. Cross the stream on a gated footbridge then go half left across the field. Go through a gate then cross the river on a wooden bridge.

You are now joining the **Ribble Way**, which runs beside the River Ribble for 70 miles (113km) from the Dales to the sea. For part of its length, north of Horton in Ribblesdale, it follows the same route as the Dales Way, another long distance footpath that goes the 80 miles (129km) from Ilkley in West Yorkshire to Bowness-on-Windermere in Cumbria.

Turn right along the riverbank, over a ladder stile, passing over a boardwalk and through woodland. Go over a stile to your right, and over a stream by a footbridge, then over another stile at its end. Continue alongside the river, going over four stiles and following the river as it bends right to a stile in a wall. Turn right over the footbridge to return to the car park.

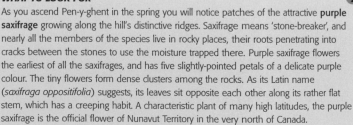

WHAT TO LOOK FOR

As you ascend Pen-y-ghent in the spring you will notice patches of the attractive **purple saxifrage** growing along the hill's distinctive ridges. Saxifrage means 'stone-breaker', and nearly all the members of the species live in rocky places, their roots penetrating into cracks between the stones to use the moisture trapped there. Purple saxifrage flowers the earliest of all the saxifrages, and has five slightly-pointed petals of a delicate purple colour. The tiny flowers form dense clusters among the rocks. As its Latin name (*saxifraga oppositifolia*) suggests, its leaves sit opposite each other along its rather flat stem, which has a creeping habit. A characteristic plant of many high latitudes, the purple saxifrage is the official flower of Nunavut Territory in the very north of Canada.

Along the Canal at Gargrave

Following the Leeds and Liverpool Canal from Gargrave.

•DISTANCE•	3½ miles (5.7km)
•MINIMUM TIME•	1hr 30min
•ASCENT / GRADIENT•	114ft (35m)
•LEVEL OF DIFFICULTY•	
•PATHS•	Field paths and tracks, then canal tow path, 4 stiles
•LANDSCAPE•	Farmland and canal side
•SUGGESTED MAP•	aqua3 OS Outdoor Leisure 2 Yorkshire Dales – Southern & Western
•START / FINISH•	Grid reference: SD 931539
•DOG FRIENDLINESS•	Dogs should be on leads, except on the canal bank
•PARKING•	Opposite church in Gargrave or in village centre
•PUBLIC TOILETS•	By bridge in Gargrave

BACKGROUND TO THE WALK

Gargrave has long been a stopping-off point for travellers from the cities of West Yorkshire on their way to the coast at Morecambe or to the Lake District. These days, most of them arrive along the A65 from Skipton, the route formerly taken by horse-drawn coaches. There is still evidence of the village's importance as a coaching centre, especially at the Old Swan Inn. Its position beside the River Aire had also proved important when 18th- and 19th-century surveyors were seeking westward routes for other methods of transport. The walk crosses the railway not long after leaving Gargrave; this is the route that, not far west, becomes the famous Settle-to-Carlisle line. And you will return to the village beside the Leeds and Liverpool Canal.

Earlier Settlers, Mills and Bandages

Although Gargrave is today mostly a 19th-century settlement, there is evidence that the area has been in occupation much longer. The site of a Roman villa has been identified nearby, while on West Street, excavation has found the remains of a moated homestead dating from the 13th century, with a smithy and a lime pit, that was reused in the 15th century. By the 18th century there were cotton mills in Gargrave, served by the canal, and weavers were engaged in producing cloth for the clothing industry. Their expertise resulted in the establishment here of one of the village's biggest employers, Johnson & Johnson Medical, where they found workers who could undertake the fine weaving that was needed to produce their bandages.

Canal Digging

In October 1774 the eastern arm of the Leeds and Liverpool canal, snaking its way westwards from Leeds, reached Gargrave. The route, surveyed by John Longbotham and approved by the great canal-builder James Brindley, had been agreed in 1770. Work began at both the Liverpool and the Leeds ends, but there were, inevitably, arguments between the separate committees in Yorkshire and Lancashire about both the route and the finances. It was not until 1810 that the canal had crossed the Pennines, and barges could go from

Leeds to Blackburn, and only in 1816 was the full distance of 127 miles (204km) open to Liverpool. Gargrave benefited not only from the access it gave the village to the raw materials for the cotton mills and the chance to export its cloth, but also as a stopping-place for the bargees.

The walk joins the canal near the lowest of the six locks at Bank Newton, where the canal begins a serpentine course to gain height as it starts its trans-Pennine journey. Near the lock is the former canal company boatyard where boats for maintaining the canal were built. As you walk along the tow path you will cross the Priest Holme Aqueduct, where the canal passes over the River Aire.

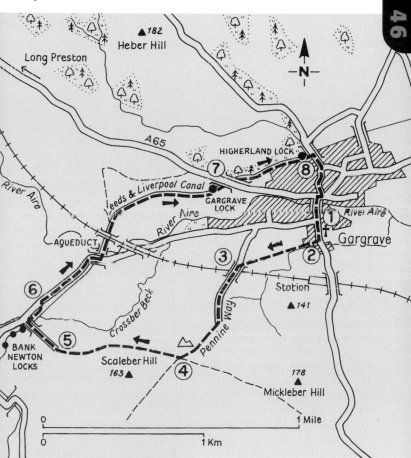

Walk 46 Directions

① Walk along the road with the church tower on your left. Just past **Church Close House** on your right, turn right, following the **Pennine Way** sign. Go over a stone stile in the wall on your left.

② Follow the side of the wall, along the Pennine Way path, which is partly boarded and partly paved here. Go ahead across the field to a waymarked stile, then half left to another stile. Walk towards the top left-hand corner of the field to a stile that leads to Mosber Lane near a railway bridge.

Walk 46

③ Turn left, going over a bridge over the railway, then follow the track through a gateway and climb the hill. After the cattle grid, go half right off the track and across the field to meet another track, which leads to a signpost.

④ At the post, turn right, soon to walk below the wire fence, to reach a waymarked gate in a crossing fence. Go ahead across the field to a pair of gates. Take the waymarked left-hand one and continue ahead, at first with a fence on your right. Follow the track through two gateways into a lane.

⑤ Follow the lane between a wall and a fence to descend to the canal by **Bank Newton Locks**. Cross the bridge and turn right along the tow path. The path passes through a gate and goes on to a road.

⑥ Go ahead along the roadside, cross the bridge over the canal then turn right down the winding path under the bridge and continue

along the tow path. Pass over a small aqueduct over the river, then under a railway bridge to reach **Gargrave Lock**.

⑦ Beyond the lock, opposite the Anchor Inn, go under the road bridge and continue along the tow path to reach **Bridge 170**, at **Higherland Lock**. Go on to the road by a signpost.

⑧ Turn right down the road, and follow it through the village, past **Gargrave Village Hall**. At the main road turn right, cross the road and go left over the bridge back to the church and the parking place.

Walk 47

Erratic Progress

From Austwick along ancient tracks to see the famous Norber Erratics.

•DISTANCE•	5½ miles (9km)
•MINIMUM TIME•	2hrs 30min
•ASCENT / GRADIENT•	558ft (170m) ▲▲▲
•LEVEL OF DIFFICULTY•	🚶🚶 🚶🚶 🚶
•PATHS•	Field and moorland paths tracks, lanes on return, 10 stiles
•LANDSCAPE•	Farmland and limestone upland
•SUGGESTED MAP•	aqua3 OS Outdoor Leisure 2 Yorkshire Dales – Southern & Central
•START / FINISH•	Grid reference: SD 767684
•DOG FRIENDLINESS•	Dogs should be on leads
•PARKING•	Roadside parking in Austwick village
•PUBLIC TOILETS•	None on route

BACKGROUND TO THE WALK

There is nothing showy about Austwick village. A pleasant, grey-built village, it has several old cottages, many of them dated in the traditional Dales way by a decorative lintel above the main door, showing the initials of the couple who had it built, together with the year they moved in. They mostly date from around the end of the 17th century. On the green in the centre is the restored market cross. The market itself, lost centuries ago to nearby Clapham, has not been restored.

Robin Proctor and Nappa

The walk takes you up Town Head Lane from the village, and across fields into Thwaite Lane. To your left is the ridge of limestone called Robin Proctor's Scar, named after a local farmer whose horse was trained to bring him home after a long night spent in the local pub. One night, too drunk to tell, he mounted the wrong horse, and it plunged over the crag with the farmer on its back. The area below the scar was formerly a tarn, and is now home to a wide variety of marsh plants. Nappa Scar, which the walk passes after you have visited the Norber Erratics, is on the North Craven Fault line. The path goes along a ledge below a steep cliff. In the cliff wall you can see the different strata of rock, including mixed conglomerate and limestone.

The Norber Erratics are world-famous. To geologists they are a place of pilgrimage, and even the non-specialist can tell that something odd is going on here. When you arrive on the plateau above Nappa Scar, you find an extensive grass-covered area, with the remnants of a limestone pavement poking through the tufts. Strewn all over the pavement are grey boulders, some of them of huge size, perched on limestone plinths. These are the erratics. Blocks of ancient greywacke stone, they were carried here from Crummackdale, more than half a mile (800m) away, by the power of a glacier, and dumped when the ice retreated. Over the centuries, the elements have worn down the limestone pavement on which they stand – except where the erratics protected it, resulting in their elevated position.

After you cross Crummack Lane and walk though fields with a limestone ridge and ancient agricultural enclosures, you will reach Austwick Beck, where the water is crossed by an ancient clapper bridge – flat stones laid across the steam from bank to bank. This leads into a walled lane that takes you to the hamlet of Wharfe. The route returns to Austwick along other walled lanes. These are the remains of old monastic ways that linked the granges, high on the fells, to the monasteries like Fountains Abbey which owned the vast sheep walks.

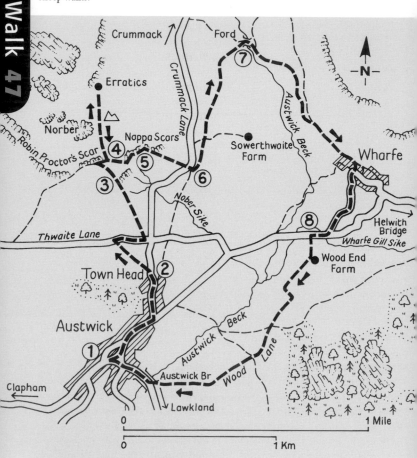

Walk 47 **Directions**

① From the triangular green in the centre of the **Austwick** village, walk northwards out of the village, following the signpost to **Horton in Ribblesdale**. Pass the **Gamecock Inn** and, just past a cottage called **Hob's Gate,** turn left up **Town Head Lane**. Just after the road bends round to the right, go left over a waymarked ladder stile.

② Walk through the field to another stile, and on to another stile on to a lane. Turn right. Just before reaching a metalled road, turn left over a ladder stile and follow the line of the track. As the track veers left, go straight on, following the line of the stone wall to a stone stile by a gate.

③ Go through the gate and continue along the rocky track. Where the stone wall on your left

Walk 47

WHILE YOU'RE THERE ⓘ

Clapham village, which stole Austwick's market, has a beck flowing through its centre, and is surrounded by attractive woodland. The village blacksmith at the end of the 18th century was James Faraday, father of the scientist Michael Faraday. From here, too, came the botanist Reginald Farrer, whose name appears in the Latin names of many of the plant species he discovered.

bends left, by a very large boulder across the path, go right on a track to pass the right-hand edge of the scar. When you reach a signpost, go left, signposted 'Norber'.

④ Follow the path uphill, to the plateau, and explore the **Norber Erratics**. Return the same way, back to the signpost. Turn left, following the sign to **Crummack**. Follow the track as it winds downhill then up beside a wall by the scar to a stone stile on your right.

⑤ Descend to another stile and follow the path beneath a rocky outcrop, which goes downhill with a wall to the left to reach a ladder stile on to a metalled lane. Cross the lane and go over another ladder stile opposite.

⑥ Turn left across the field. Go over two ladder stiles, cross a farm track and go over a ridge of rock to a stone stile then a ladder stile. Go over the stile and on to the track. Turn right and cross the ford on a clapper bridge.

⑦ Follow the track between the walls for ½ mile (800m) into **Wharfe**. Turn left by the bridleway sign in the village, then follow the road round to the right and go down the village approach road to reach a metalled road. Turn right. After 100yds (91m) turn left at a bridleway sign to **Wood Lane**, down the road to **Wood End Farm**.

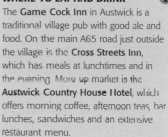

WHERE TO EAT AND DRINK ⓘ

The **Game Cock Inn** in Austwick is a traditional village pub with good ale and food. On the main A65 road just outside the village is the **Cross Streets Inn**, which has meals at lunchtimes and in the evening. More up market is the **Austwick Country House Hotel**, which offers morning coffee, afternoon teas, bar lunches, sandwiches and an extensive restaurant menu.

⑧ By the farm buildings the track goes right. Follow it as it bends left and right to a crossroads of tracks. Go straight ahead, following the line of telegraph poles. The track winds to reach the metalled lane into the village. Turn right over the bridge to the village centre.

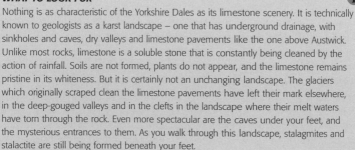

WHAT TO LOOK FOR ⓘ

Nothing is as characteristic of the Yorkshire Dales as its limestone scenery. It is technically known to geologists as a karst landscape – one that has underground drainage, with sinkholes and caves, dry valleys and limestone pavements like the one above Austwick. Unlike most rocks, limestone is a soluble stone that is constantly being cleaned by the action of rainfall. Soils are not formed, plants do not appear, and the limestone remains pristine in its whiteness. But it is certainly not an unchanging landscape. The glaciers which originally scraped clean the limestone pavements have left their mark elsewhere, in the deep-gouged valleys and in the clefts in the landscape where their melt waters have torn through the rock. Even more spectacular are the caves under your feet, and the mysterious entrances to them. As you walk through this landscape, stalagmites and stalactite are still being formed beneath your feet.

Around Ribblehead's Majestic Viaduct

Beside and beneath a great monument to Victorian engineering.

•DISTANCE•	5 miles (8km)
•MINIMUM TIME•	2hrs
•ASCENT / GRADIENT•	328ft (100m) ▲▲▲
•LEVEL OF DIFFICULTY•	🚶 🚶 🚶
•PATHS•	Moorland and farm paths and tracks, 2 stiles
•LANDSCAPE•	Bleak moorland and farmland, dominated by the Ribblehead viaduct
•SUGGESTED MAP•	aqua3 OS Outdoor Leisure 2 Yorkshire Dales – Western
•START / FINISH•	Grid reference: SD 765792
•DOG FRIENDLINESS•	Dogs can be off lead by viaduct, but should be on leads in farmland
•PARKING•	Parking space at junction of B6255 and B6479 near Ribblehead viaduct
•PUBLIC TOILETS•	None on route

BACKGROUND TO THE WALK

'Nowhere in the kingdom has nature placed such gigantic obstacles in the way of the railway engineer', observed a newspaper when the Settle-to-Carlisle railway line was complete. The railway was planned and built by the Midland Railway so it could reach Scotland without trespassing on its rivals' territory of the east or west coast routes. It cost the then enormous sum of £3,500,000 and was opened in 1876. Its construction included building 20 big viaducts and 14 tunnels. At the height of the works, 6,000 men were employed, living in shanty towns beside the line and giving the area a flavour of the Wild West. The line survived for almost 100 years, until passenger services were withdrawn in 1970. It was said that the viaducts, especially the Ribblehead, were unsafe. There was a public outcry which led to a concerted campaign to keep the line open. Since then there has been a change of heart. Ribblehead is repaired, and the line is one of the most popular – and spectacular – tourist lines in the country.

Ribblehead – 'A Mighty Work'

It took all of five years to build Ribblehead's huge viaduct. It is a quarter of a mile (400m) long, and is 100ft (30m) high at its maximum; the columns stretch another 25ft (7.6m) into the ground. The stone – more than 30,000 cubic yards (22,950 cubic m) of it – came from Littledale to the north, and construction progressed from north to south. The area is called Batty Moss, and was inhospitable, to say the least. There is a rumour that the columns are set on bales of wool, as the engineers could not find the bedrock. This, romantic as it is in a county whose fortunes are largely based in wool, is untrue; they are set in concrete on top of the rock below. There are 24 spans, each 45ft (13.7m) wide. Every sixth column is thicker than its neighbours so that if one column fell it would take only five others with it, and not the whole viaduct.

Walk 48

Blea Moor and Ancient Farms

The walk takes you past the viaduct to the beginning of Blea Moor, and near perhaps the most exposed signal box in Britain. Beyond it is Blea Moor tunnel, another of the mighty engineering works of the Settle-to-Carlisle Railway, 2,629yds (2,400m) long and dug by miners working by candlelight. They got through £50-worth of candles each month. The advent of the miners and the huge paraphernalia of Victorian engineering must have seemed astonishing to the farmers sheltering at the foot of Whernside. With their ancient, Norse-inspired names – Winterscales, Broadrake, Gunnerfleet – their farms are an enduring testimony to the resilience of man long before he tried to tame it with such forces.

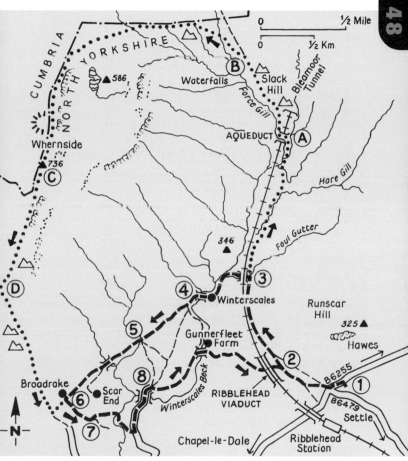

Walk 48 Directions

① From the parking place, cross the road and take the boardwalk by the sign towards the viaduct to a track. Turn right and follow the track until it turns under the viaduct; continue straight ahead.

② Continue walking, now parallel with the railway line above you to your left. Go past a **Three Peaks** signboard, following the **Whernside** sign. Go over a gated wooden stile and continue until you reach a railway signal. Go left under the railway arch, following the public bridleway sign.

Walk 48

③ Go through a gate at the end of the arch and follow the track downhill towards the stream, then bear left towards farm buildings. Go through a gate between the buildings and on to a humpback bridge by a cottage.

④ Follow the lane over two cattle grids, through a wooden gate by a barn, then through a metal gate, to wind through the farm buildings. Go through another metal gate then a waymarked wooden gate.

⑤ Walk along a track through the fields, going over a small bridge of railway sleepers. By a sign to **Scar End**, bear right to a small gate. Go across three fields, through a series of gates and continue ahead through the next field, to reach farm buildings.

⑥ Turn left by the farm down the farm track. Where it bends right, go over the cattle grid and turn sharp left round the fence and on to a track, following the bridleway sign, to a ladder stile.

⑦ The obvious track winds through fields to reach a stream bed (dry in summer). Cross this, and continue along the track to meet a road near a cattle grid. Turn left and walk down the road and over a bridge.

⑧ Where the road divides, go right, through a gate, towards the viaduct. At the next gate go right again over a footbridge by the farm buildings. Continue through two more gates and follow the track under the viaduct, continuing towards the road and the parking place.

Ribblehead and Whernside Summit

If you want to explore the Ribblehead area further, this extension takes you to the summit of Whernside and back.

See map and information panel for Walk 48

•DISTANCE•	7¼ miles (11.7km)
•MINIMUM TIME•	3hrs 30min
•ASCENT / GRADIENT•	1,673ft (510m) ▲▲▲
•LEVEL OF DIFFICULTY•	🚶 🚶 🚶

Walk 49 Directions (Walk 48 option)

At Point ③ on the main walk, do not turn under the railway arch, but go straight ahead, signposted to **Dent**. Pass **Blea Moor signal box**. The track crosses over two streams and goes alongside an aqueduct (Point Ⓐ), where the railway engineers have provided a new channel to take the waters of the **Force Gill** over the railway line. Go over a stile, and at a signpost continue ahead to **Dentdale**.

This is part of the **Craven Way**, formerly a packhorse track linking **Ribblesdale** and **Dentdale**. The path ascends to a stile, with a waterfall to the left, then climbs steeply to reach another stile on your left, Point Ⓑ.

Turn left over the stile, following the **Whernside** sign. The wall on the right is the North Yorkshire County boundary. The path is paved in parts as it crosses the bog, and ascends towards the summit of **Whernside**. To the right are views of **Dent Head** viaduct and the

ventilation shafts for the **Blea Moor tunnel**, while further along there are views to the Howgill Fells. At the summit (Point Ⓒ), continue along the same path, with the wall on your right, and descend to a stile by a signpost. The footpath then goes down two sets of steep, rough steps, to reach two ladder stiles over a wall.

Continue to descend to reach a place where the path swings away from the wall, Point Ⓓ. Follow the path steeply downhill to reach two ladder stiles over a wall, and continue to another pair of ladder stiles by a farm gate, followed by a single ladder stile. After the farm gate beside a barn, turn left, signed 'Winterscales'. Follow the path through the field towards the farm. Go through a gate to reach Point ⑥ on the main walk. Turn right down the farm track.

WHERE TO EAT AND DRINK ℹ️

In the summer months an **ice cream van** stations itself at the Ribblehead viaduct car park, and **Winterscales Farm** sometimes offers teas. The **Station Inn**, near the viaduct, offers warmth (the wind blows at Ribblehead!) and home-cooked meals in its bar and dining room.

Ingleton and its Famous Waterfalls

A classic Dales walk by the waterfalls, on a route first devised in 1885.

•DISTANCE•	5 miles (8km)
•MINIMUM TIME•	2hrs
•ASCENT / GRADIENT•	689ft (210m) ▲ ▲ ▲
•LEVEL OF DIFFICULTY•	🚶 🚶 🚶
•PATHS•	Good paths and tracks, 1 stile
•LANDSCAPE•	Two wooded valleys with waterfalls, and section of ancient track with wide views
•SUGGESTED MAP•	aqua3 OS Outdoor Leisure 2 Yorkshire Dales – Southern & Central
•START / FINISH•	Grid reference: SD 693733
•DOG FRIENDLINESS•	Dogs should be on leads by waterfalls
•PARKING•	Car park in centre of Ingleton, or at start of Falls Walk
•PUBLIC TOILETS•	Ingleton

Walk 50 **Directions**

From the car park in the centre of Ingleton, follow the **Waterfalls Walk signs**, which take you downhill and across the river to the Waterfalls entrance. Walk through the Waterfalls car park and go through two kissing gates. The path goes downwards at first, then ascends steps.

This is **Swilla Glen**, where you first get a taste of what is to come on the

---

WHILE YOU'RE THERE ⓘ

Further up the valley, to the north east of Ingleton, is the hamlet of **Chapel-le-Dale**, beautifully set beside the River Greta. Its tiny church – less than 50ft (15m) from end to end – may have been built in the 17th century; no one seems quite sure. In the churchyard are the graves of some of the navvies who died during the construction of the Settle-to-Carlisle Railway.

---

walk. The **River Twiss** here passes through a deep gorge, with rapids and whirlpools. Cross **Manor Bridge** and continue upstream. **Pecca Bridge** returns you to the left bank of the stream, by **Pecca Falls**, where the river tumbles over a shelf of the hard greywacke stone, eating away at the softer slate beds below.

Continue to follow the path uphill to **Thornton Force**. Unlike the other falls on the walk, Thornton Force is not a series of rapids confined within the valley, but plunges 40ft (12.2m) into a deep pool gouged into the slate beds below, which have been heaved into a vertical bed. This is one of the classic spots for studying the geology of the area. Below the lip of hard limestone are the different strata, including the slates and more greywacke. The path winds slightly away from the stream and up steps, then takes you over **Ravenray Bridge**, and up more steps to a

---

WHERE TO EAT AND DRINK ⓘ

As you would expect, Ingleton is well-served with places to eat and drink. There are refreshments available at the entrance to the **Waterfalls Walk**. Among the cafés are **Bernies**, which also sells gear for walkers, climbers and cavers, **Fountain Café** and **Curlew Crafts and Tea Rooms**. **Inglenook Chippy** serves traditional fish and chips, and also has a café. The best of the pubs is the **Wheatsheaf**, which serves good meals.

---

kissing gate on to a lane. Turn right along **Twisleton Lane**, an ancient packhorse route. Above you are **Twisleton Scars**, great bands of limestone interspersed with horizontal bands of shale. One of the best limestone pavements in the area is to be found at the top of the Scars. Go through two gates, and the track becomes metalled. Walk past the farm buildings, following **Waterfalls Walk** signs. On the opposite hillside you will see the entrance building for **White Scar Caves**, discovered in 1923 and one of the best of the Dales' show caves, with vast caverns containing massive (and imaginatively-named) stalagmites and stalactites. Go over a gated stone stile and along the track. A kissing gate takes you on to a road. Go straight across, signed 'Skirwith'. The path goes right, following a Waterfall Walk sign, through a metal handgate, then through a kissing gate into woodland. This is the valley of the **River Greta**. The woodland here is some of the oldest and most unspoiled in the area, with ancient oak trees flanking the waterfalls.

The path passes **Beezley Falls**, with its three separate channels, and **Rival Falls**. A little further down, a path to the left takes you to a footbridge with a good view of the deep and narrow **Baxenghyll Gorge**. Continue to follow the path which takes you over a footbridge, through a kissing gate, then past former quarry workings. These were limestone quarries, and their remains still scar the landscape. Quarrying is still carried out around Ingleton; the largest workings are cutting away the hillside to provide road stone.

Go ahead through a handgate on to a lane, and follow it into the centre of **Ingleton**. A workaday town, and one of the Dales' honeypots, Ingleton shows its mining and quarrying history in its buildings. It became a place for tourists to visit when the railway arrived in 1859 – the viaduct almost cuts the village in half. The entrepreneurs who developed the Waterfalls Walk in the 1880s, and charged for the privilege of taking the route, were tapping into the start of one of the most profitable of Dales industries. Turn right past the church – worth visiting for its Norman font – and back to the car park.

WHAT TO LOOK FOR ⓘ

Once growing in profusion in the area, the **Lady's Slipper orchid** is one of the rarest of Britain's endangered plants. It died out largely because of people digging plants up to put in their gardens, or taking the flowers for their collections of pressed specimens. English Nature has now reintroduced this beautiful plant, which has large maroon-coloured flowers, with a yellow lip and red spots inside – resembling the footwear which gives it its common name. Its leaves are pale green, with definite ribs to them. It is a characteristic plant of open woodland like that beside the waterfalls. Seeds were propagated at Kew Gardens, and the seedlings were planted in a protected area beside the Ingleton Waterfalls Walk, so that visitors can see their progress.

Walking in Safety

All these walks are suitable for any reasonably fit person, but less experienced walkers should try the easier walks first. Route finding is usually straightforward, but you will find that an Ordnance Survey map is a useful addition to the route maps and descriptions.

Risks

Although each walk here has been researched with a view to minimising the risks to the walkers who follow its route, no walk in the countryside can be considered to be completely free from risk. Walking in the outdoors will always require a degree of common sense and judgement to ensure that it is as safe as possible.

- Be particularly careful on cliff paths and in upland terrain, where the consequences of a slip can be very serious.

- Remember to check tidal conditions before walking on the seashore.

- Some sections of route are by, or cross, busy roads. Take care and remember traffic is a danger even on minor country lanes.

- Be careful around farmyard machinery and livestock, especially if you have children with you.

- Be aware of the consequences of changes in the weather and check the forecast before you set out. Carry spare clothing and a torch if you are walking in the winter months. Remember the weather can change very quickly at any time of the year, and in moorland and heathland areas, mist and fog can make route finding much harder. Don't set out in these conditions unless you are confident of your navigation skills in poor visibility. In summer remember to take account of the heat and sun; wear a hat and carry spare water.

- On walks away from centres of population you should carry a whistle and survival bag. If you do have an accident requiring the emergency services, make a note of your position as accurately as possible and dial 999.

Acknowledgements

The author would like to thank those who helped with the preparation of this book, and especially Karen Snowden of the Rotunda Museum, Scarborough; Rona Charles, Ecologist at the North York Moors National Park; the Yorkshire Wildlife Trust; Yorkshire Water: the libraries in Ripon and York; the proprietors of several guest houses throughout the county; and the other walkers met en route.

To Sheila, who provided encouragement, sandwiches and common sense; to Tom, who stayed at home; and to Ben who shared much of the walking and got me organised.,

Series management: Outcrop Publishing Services, Cumbria
Series editor: Chris Bagshaw
Front cover: AA Photo Library/J Morrison